SOCIAL CHANGE HOW INFLUENCES SERVICE NEED CHANGE

JOHN LOK

Made with ♥ on the Notion Press Platform
www.notionpress.com

Contents

Preface

Introduction

Our business society had developed long time from farming period to manufacturing period, then to service industry period, till to nowadays technology service and manufacturing period. It brings this question: Can technology or human behavior may influence economic development? How social change may influence service need change?

In my this book, I give examples to explain how to apply psychological and behavioral economic both view point related methods to predict individual service need behavioral change to let businessmen learn how to choose the reasonable or right methods to attract customers to choose the kind of service in preference.

Prologue

Contents

How and why employees behaviors may influence economy development?
Robots invention whether they can help organizations to raise efficiencies or inefficiencies?
Why social behavior may influence organizational strategy needs to be changed ?
How and why human behavior may influence economic growth or recession?
Reasons why human behavior may influence economic recession or growth ?
How employee behavior influences organizational development?
p.39-50

Chapter 2 How social chance influences Disney visitor leisure need change

Apply knowledge management method to predict Walt Disney entertainment theme park behavioral consumption p.51-69

Disney market research method

Brand image attention of behavioral consumption of prediction method

Can scientific research method predict Disney visitors behavior ?

Can intentions Disney visitor behavior be predicted by survey research ?

Chapter 3 How social change influences student school choice

University campus choice and teaching method choice psychological prediction

University campus location factor p.70-83

The resource based theory of university
location competitive advantage
The factor of student demand for
alternative modes of course delivery

Whether online and hybrid courses will
influence to university students to choose

the university to study.

Chapter 4 How social change influences airline passenger need change

How to predict passenger individual consumption choice for airline industry p.84-100

How can airline gas or oil price influence passenger individual airline choice?

What is the relationship of oil price and terrorism to airline industry to influence ticket price increasing?

How can demand be caused by e-service transaction channel to predict passenger individual consumption choice for airline industry?

Can advertising influence consumption behavior?

How can airline atmosphere environment influence traveller travel choice behavior?

How can airline counter servicer knowledge influence traveller consumption behavior?

In -store consumer digital signage behavior how can influence consumer behavior

CHAPTER ONE

How social change influences consumer behavior change

Human Behavioral network job brings social economic benefits

What does human network job mean ? Why may human network job be popular? Why human network job behavior may influence economy ?

Nowadays internet is popular to use. We can apply internet to find data , search any new things, even earn money. Why does internet may become huma network job source. For example, e-publish may be one kind of new human network job. Any authors may apply internet

channel to help them to sell electronic or paper books from e-publisher web store. They may apply facebook, you tub etc. any online

channel to promote themselves new books to let new readers to know whether when they may buy themselves favourable new topic books to read

from electronic publisher web store.

Thus, future electronic publisher industry may help any authors to build internet network platform to help them to sell and promote ot advertise their any one new electronic or paper book topic to let global any one reader to choose to buy their any new topic books from electronic publisher web store easily and conveniently. However, it implies that electronic network platform author may be one kind of future new human network job in our societies.

How electronic network platform author job may bring economy benefit in macro economy view? A person can have few friends, contacts and still be very influential if these few
friends and contacts are themselves highly influential, e.g. one author must not need to know any one reader in global society. When they like to choose any electronic books from electronic internet network platform. They may become the author's any one topic book buyer, when they feel the author's any one topic book is fun and attract they make decision to buth the strange author whose the topic book from electronic book publisher's platform web store conventiently in short time. Although, they are strangers, they do not know themselves , but the reader can understand what it way that made Google from writing platofrm to create new creative mind and typing network job method to replace traditional hand writing book method for global authors. It will be one kind of new human network writing job.

Hence, global any one reader can apply an innovative search engine , such as google.com to find whether whom author personal new topic books are value to read from internet.
Then, the electroniuc publisher's web store may be new book store platform sale network to help the author to sell many electronic or paper books from electronic network platform
in short time. So, internet may be future new network plaform to help global any one author to create network writing job absolutely. Furthermore, internet may be popular social media
to help any one author to build goold relationship between his/ her readers. It is one kind of new network, human network job. New authors do not need to buy many paper books to prepare to put in any one book shop warehouse. Their every book can print on demand to reduce out of book stock in any one book shop.

They may choose to sell either electronic books or paper books both from any one book publisher web store. So, electronic network platform may be one kind of good writing channel to help human authors to create income and it can also help authors to bring new creative mind and new topic fun content books to let readers to know and buy to read from electronic publisher network platform.

Why does human behavior may be one kind of new human network job to bring global economic advantages. ALthough, it may be free income or without inocme, but the person does the network behavior, his/her behavior may be bring advantages to influence many other people's health. For this case, when a worker in a coffee shop in an airport gets a vaccination aganinst the flu, it does not only helps him or her stay healthy, but also helps the many travellers who might otherwise have been inflected if that workers caught the flu. So, the externality , the result implies the vaccination of even a part of a community conveys benefits to the whole community. For example, governments pay special attention to the vaccinations of school children, teachers, health mothers, and the elderly, categories of people particularly susceptible not only to catching, but also to transmitting a disease.

It is not accidential that governments are heavily involved with vaccination . When there are externalities, free market, fail to persuade individual incentives with society's

their the worker's decision of whether to get a vaccine ends up attracting whether other people get sick. The workers might not fully take all these other people's potential suffering into account when making her or his vaccination decision.

As Stanford University does many suggestions, understand this and tries to help them make the right decisions and so providers free flu vaccines for its staff and students.

Small pockets of unvaccinated individuals can allow a disease to gain a spread more widely well-being. For example, parent weighing the costs and benefits of a vaccine for their child is not always thinking of the consequences of that vaccination to other people. THese are markets in which subsidizing or regulating behavior can make everyone better off. Because the reason for requiring that a child be vaccinated before enrolling in school is not just to protect that child, because each child's vaccination affects others via potential contagions.

Robots take our jobs behavioral and economy influences

Robot job behavior brings economy influences

If one day robots can replace human to do simple, even complex jobs. They will bring what influences to our global societial economy.The popular economic refrain declares that the global middle class is dying and robots will soon take our jobs, e.g. shopping center customer service jobs, library service jobs, cinema ticket sale jobs, restaurant kitchen cooker jobs, even, bus drivers, taxi drivers etc. public transport driving jobs, accountant, doctors etc. professional jobs. Whether it is beautiful or petty matter if our future societies have many human jobs can be replaced to do from robots. Businessman must may reduce to employ employees and reduce to pay salary or wage, when robots can be replaced to do their employees tasks. But, societies must bring unemployement rate rises , due to societies will have many people loss jobs when their employers choose to buy robots to serve their clients or do any office tasks or customer service or cleaning etc. tasks.

In micro economy view, employers may save money in long term, but in macro economy view, it will cause unemployment ratio rises , even crime rate rises when there are many people lose jobs in societies. These models of doom, though, fail to account for the hundreds of businesses riding the waves of change in their industries when robots may be invented to replace human to do many simple , even complex tasks in our future societies.

WE may image that one small factory needs to manufacture fishes canes to sell to supermarket, the small , cheaper stuff and higher margin parts of the fishes manufacture industry. Before, this factory needs to employe many human factory workers need to help every fresh customer makeing the perfect fishing gear, designed for performance, durability, and cost in order to achieve to manufacture every fish cane in whole fished processing manufacturing stages. Every worker needs to spend about 15 to twenty minutes to finish every fish cane , till to delivery to any supermarket to sell. If this fish canes manufacturing factory can apply manufacturing robots to help them to finish any one working tasks , every robot can only spend five minutes to finish whole fresh fish cane manufacturing process. Thus, every robot can

help this factory save 10 to 15 minutes time to finsh every fish cane manufacturing process. IN fact, time is money, because when every robot can help this factory to reduce 10 to 15 minutes time to compare human worker. Then, this factory can finish about 20 fish canes in one hour if it can use robot to help it to manufacture fish canes. Otherwise, if this factory still use human workers to help it to manufacture fish canes, then it can finsh about 3 to 4 fish canes in one hour. SO, the manufacturing efficiency ensures that robots must help this fish manufacturing factory to raise fish canes number more than human workers. So, in robotic behavioral economy view, manufacturing robots must help this fish canes manufacturing factory to raise fish canes manufacturing number and deliver increasing number to supermarkets to prepare to sell every day. Robots can help this fish canes manufacturing factory bring manufacturing time saving, rising manufacturing efficiency, improving performance and reducing wages expenditure long time advantages in micro economy view. However, manufacturing robots can also bring disadvanages to society, e.g. increasing unemployment ratio, increasing crime rate,

this factory workers will lose jobs and income, they need earn social welfare from government and increasing government finance pressure in short time, even long time in macro economic view.

Stanford University graduate program in economics, Scott lecturer explained that "in demand and supply economic theory for robots supply and demand case, robots supply number increasing may influence human workers demand number decrease. It sometimes calls " the efficient frontier".

No specific human beings were mentioned in any of economics classes. As robots supply and demand in market case, They (robots) may be purely theoretical " agents" who reached to the most reasonable sale prices in order to persuade any one businessman buyer to make manufacturing robot buying decision whether robots can help him / her to bring how much saving time , saving money, saving cost, improving performance, efficiency economic benefit before he/she plans to reduce workers number when he/she decides to apply robots to replace human workers in his/her factory or office or any service department, e.g. cinema ticket sale service, shopping center customer service, shopping center cleaning , supermarket customer service etc. service or sale tasks. When robots can replace human to do any one of these tasks in any organizations. So, robots may be human worker agents who reached to prices the way robots would react to a software command. There was nothing that explained why some people thrived and others did n't or why truly brilliant, hardworking people could fail when much lazier folks succeeded." Having been admitted to the Stanford University graduate program in economics, Scott lecturer hoped to get his answers there.

How robots influence our future social changing? Using the right technology can be a boon to your business in this economy. For internet example, it is easier than ever to find well-matched customers all around the world, to stay in contact with them, and to more quickly design the products they want. If you focus solely on being cutting -edge, though you risk letting the technology take over what should be very robust relationships with your customers , employees, and colleagues. IN nowaddays society, technoligical advances and cutomation, personal relationships in business are more crucial than ever. I mean that robots can not replace human to serve clients to let them to feel more comfortable and passion more easily. For shoe shop case example, if the shoe shop apply one robot to serve its clients to replace human shoe salesperson to serve its shoe customers. Robots ensure that they can not persuade every shoe potential buyer to make shoe buying decision more easily when robots need to contact every shoe potential buyer. The reason is simple, because robots can not touch any one shoe buyer individual emotion very easier. If the shoe buyer needs the robots to help him/her to choose any right shoe styles when he/she can not feel himself / herself can make the most right shoe style choice decision. The robots can not replace human shoe salesperson to make shoe style choice judgement more easily. They must need longer time to analyze whether which shoe style may be the most suitable to the shoe buyer. Otherwise, human shoe salesperson may attempt to make the most right shoe style choice decision to help any one shoe buyer to chooce the most right style shoe because he/she owns shoe style sale experience, shoe style knowledge, the most important reason is that they can feel every shoe customer individual emotion to touch whether he/she will feel comfortable or happy when they attempt to help every shoe customer to seek the most right shoe style in every shoe customer whole shoe searching processing. Othwerwise, serving robots are only one machine, they can not touch or feel every shoe customer individual emotion whether he/she feel comfortable or unhappy or happy when they need to contact them in whole shoe searching processing. Hence, I believe that some tasks robots can

not repalce human staff to do very easily. Otherwise, robots may bring disadvanatges to let any one businessman to loss his/her customers, due to robots can not touch every customer

emotion to compare human staff in service tasks more easily. Robots serving customer behaviors may cause money lose and customers number lose to the shop in micro economic view.

Intellectual human economic behaviors

What does intellectual human economic behaviors mean ? I believe that when we choose or decide to do intellectual behaviors, then our societies will be influenced to bring economic growth in consequence.I shall attempt to indicate pollution case to explain how and why eithet our intellectual or foolish behaviors may bring economic growth or recession in consequence as below:

On one hand, for air pollution social case aspect example, if we only consider to buy cars to drive for working aimr or holiday leisure aim. Then, our societies air will be polluted. Our health will be influenced to bad. Our car driving behaviors may cause global environment air pollution serously. In long tiem, global air pollution will bring our bodies health to be bad. Although, ourselves car driving behaviors may bring our driving travelling leisure enjoyment and comfortable feeling in short time, also we so not need to pay public transport fare often, but we need to compensate ourselves health economic intangible loss due to air pollution , when cars number increases, dirty air will cause ouselves health to become bad.

In the result, we will need to pay more medical expenditure when we are old age, due to ourselves bodies will become bad, due to we breathe global dirty air every day, due to ourselves cars pollute air in long time, e.g. 10 to 20 years, even 30 more without limited air pollution environment. So, driving cars behavior may be one kind of human foolish behavior and our foolish behavior may bring ourselves future long time medical expenditure absolutely.

One the other hand, water pollution social aspect, if we often keep much rubblish to pollute sea, oil exploration porcessing pollute ocean , ships gas pollute ocaen, then fishes will eat polluted food and drive dirty water, due to global ocean is polluted.

In fact, because human only to conside how to buy boats to carry on leisure enjoyment activities, or catch cruises to travel on the sea. Also, oil manufacturers only consider researching anywhere to find new oil exploration places to manufacture oil product, when their oil exploration processes pollute ocarn . Consequently, global fishes drink polluted warer or eat polluted food. They will have poison. SO, human will have high chance to eat poison polluted fishes, due to fishes are poison or are polluted.

So, human is doing foolish activities, we only hope to find oil exploration places to pollute ocean or we only spend money to buy ticket to catch ships to travel anywhere in global ocean. All of these human foolish behaviors will bring pollution to global ocean. On consequently, we will need to compensate to eat polluted or dirty or poision fishes, ourselves bodies health will be bad. In long time, we need have high chance to pay medical expenditure when we are old. So, pollution case may be one good example to explain how and why human foolish behavior may influence ourselves future need to compensate serious medical loss.

All of these human foolish behavior will bring pollution to global ocean. On consequently, we will need to compensate to eat polluted or dirty or poison fished , ourselves bodies health will be bad. In long time, we will have high chance to pay medical expenditure, when we are old. So, pollution case may be one good example to explain how and why human ourselves intellectual or foolish behaviors may influence future long time economic loss or economic growth or recession in micro and micro economic view.

On another water pollution aspect hand, if we often keep rubbish to sea, oil exploration processing pollutes ocean and ships' gas pollute ocean, then fishes will eat polluted food and drink dirty water, due to fishes will eat polluted food and drink dirty sea water because the global ocean is polluted seriously.

In fact, because human only consider how to buy boats to carry on any leisure water activities, or catches cruises to travel on the sea. Also, oil manufacturers only consider any where to find oil exploratin places to manufacture oil products from ocean, when their pol exploration processes can plooute ocean. Consequently, global fishes drink polluted water or eat direty food. They will have poison. So, human will have high chance to eat poison fishes.

Otherwise, such as pollutin case, it can infuence inflation or deflation. Consequently, the reason indicates supply and demand theory. If air pollution is serious, then we will consider health issue, global cars demand number may be influenced to reduce, when global cars number demand will reduce, global car prices and supply number will need to change to fall down in order to attract or persuade global car consumers choose to make car purchase decision.

Hence, global car manufacture number and car price will be

influenced to reduce, due to global air pollution issue. Consequently, deflation will occur because when the country citizen usually does not spend much extra saving money to buy car expensive goods. Money value will be low. Otherwise, if global cair pollution is not serious, human considers to buy cars to enjoy driving leisure lives. So, global car demand is influenced to increase , also global car price will also influenced to increase.

Consequently, gobal human will choose to buy cars to drive. Due to we accept to spend extra saving to buy expensive car goods. Car sale price and supply may be influenced to rise up. Money value is influenced to reduce. Inflation may be influenced, due to global car consumers number increases, we would not have extra money to spend easily. Car expensive goods expenditure influences our spending habit to avoid to make car purchase decision more easily. So, human intellectual or foolish activities may bring inflation or deflation consequency in possible indirectly in macro economic view.

On conclusion, above pollution case explain that how and why human intellectual or foolish economic behaviors may bring inflation or deflation consequency as wll as economic growth or recession consequency as well as any goods demand and supply increasing or decreasing consequency. It implies that human behavior may have indirect relationship to influence any goods demand and supply number to either increase or decrease result as well as any goods price will be influenced to increase or decrease in micro and macro economic view.

The relationship between social change and human behavior

Why does economic changes may influence human individual behavioral change? I shall attempt to indicate shopping behavior and staying at home behavior to explain their case and effect relationsip as below:

Human behavior can be influenced by economic change or economic change can be influenced by human behavior? Why does recession may influence consumers reduce shopping desire? In social recession suitation, it is possible that many people lose jobs suddenly, due to businessmen lose many customers. They need to make decision to reduce employees number in order to continue to keep businesses. Consequently, many firms (organizations) their employees may lose jobs. When they have much time, due to lose jobs, they will feel to avoid to spend too much time and money to go to shopping often. Many losing jobs people, they will often stay at homes.

So, they will reduce time to go to shopping, then non essential products won't their preferable choice purchase products. Hence, recession will change many losing jobs people their shopping or consumption desires to avoid to buy non essential products often . Usually when economic boom, many people have jobs to do because consumers number must increase when many people have jobs to do. Then, many people can accept to spend money to buy non essential products often. Many people feel spend time to go to shopping can satisfy their purchase of any kinds of new products useful psychology or desire. So, recession is one good example to explain it can influence many people do not like often to leave homes to go to shopping easily. Many people like to stay at homes, becaue they feel worry about spending too much shopping time when they leave homes. Their staying home time is one good negative shopping behavior example. So, economic change may influence human individual behavior changes , they have direct cause and efect relationship in behavioral economic view.

May human behavior influence economic change? Is it possible that human behavior may bring the country social economic change in macro economic or micro behavioral economic view ? I shall indicate publishing industry example. Do you feel that if there are many students feel learning is very important when they read many books or many of students feel interesting to read or they have reading new books in habit, then it is possible that the country will have many students like to spend time to go to any book shops to choose the books, they feel that they can help they learn new knowledge. Then the country will increase students number, they often spend time to visit any one book shop every week. Their visiting book shops behavior which may become their habits. So, the country will increase students number, they often spend time to visit book shops. Also, it implies that visiting book shops behaviors may be their behavioral habits.

So, when the country has many students often spend time to visit book shops , their visiting book shops behaviors may help any one book shop to raise books sale chance. So, the country's student individual often visiting book shop behaviors, their habitual visiting book shops behaviors must may assist help any one book shop to increase books sale number absolutely.

Consequently, any one book shop , its books sale bumber must be influenced to increase to increase because the country will have many students like or feel need visit book shops habit in order to choose any suitable books to buy to read at home in order to raise themselves learning effort. When the country has many bok shops often have many students visit their book shops, then their books sale number may be influenced to increase. It explain why student individual visiting book shop behavior may help any one book shop sale number increases also.

How human productive behavior may influence economic development

May any country which citizen behavior assist themselves country development? It is one cause and effect economic question. I mean that if the country itself citicen can not concentrate mind or energy to choose to do one kind of industry in order to let themselves country can bring the most benefit, then whether the counry itself economy can bring the most serious economic benefit. I shall attempt to indicate these countries themselves indistry choice to explain whether these countries themselves citizen productive behavior may help themselves countries to achieve the largest economic benefits. I shall indicate as below:

New Zealand farmer individual wine productive behavior

For New Zealand country example, this country concerns itself effort is foucs on farming agricultural aspect. So, this country has many farmers concentrate on farming agricultural aspect. May New

Zealanders choose to spend time to produce different kinds of wines, e.g. wine or red grape wine is for the people are eating meat, or they are eating dinner.

When these New Zealanders their behaviors choose to do farming or agriculture to grow and produce different kinds of taste of white or red grape wine drinking products job. Themselves grape agriculture behavior will influence these New Zealanders themselves, they can learn how to improve different kinds of grape wine drinking products in order to achieve every kinds of white or read grape wines taste improving aim during their white or red grape producing process.

Why can New Zealander every individual white or read grape wine producers improve their white or read grape wine taste more easily? In behavioral economic view, it can explain that why any one New Zealander white or read grape wine producer can be encouraged or excited or persuaded to concentrate nervous and energy and effort to learn how to improve their white or red grape wine products easily.

In fact, New Zealand is one agricultural food export country. It has good natural environment resource , e.g. land, seed to provide any one farmer to produce themselves any kinds of agricultrual food products, e.g. fruit, or wine food products. Because New Zealanders know themselves country has enough natural resource . So, in common, many New Zealanders choose to attempt to do farming agricultural jobs in order to export themselves any kinds of fruit or meat or wine products to overseas or sell to domestic in order to earn profit.

So, when these New Zealand farmers number has been increasing every year. This country farmers will feel themsleves competition between this New Zealand farmers themselves are serious due to they may feel New Zealanders choose to do agriculture businesses in order to export themselves different kinds of farming food to overseas or sell to local to earn profit.

Hence, when many New Zealand farmers feel that farmers number has been increasing every year. They will feel themselves competition is serious. They must need to spend much time and nervous and effort to research what method is the best how to produce the best taste of white or red grape wine products in order to let local or overseas wine buyers to choose to buy his/her producing white or read grpae products to drink.

Hence, in competition psychological view, may influence many New Zealand white or reaad wine producers had been beginning to change their learning behavior on researching what method is the best in order to produce the best quality of taste red or white wine products to sell in order to attract overseas or local white or read grape wine drinkers to choose to buy his/her wine products. Their behavior will focus on learning how to raising or improving white or read grape wine taste method more than only focus on producing a large number white or red grape wine products. They believe wine quality is more important to compare wine producing number. So, New Zealand wine producers themselves wine producers behaviors have been changing on concentrating on researching wine quality method aspect more then wine producing number aspect in behavioral economic view.

America high technological productive behavior

For America example, US is one high technological country, it owns many high technological knowledge talent inventors, e.g. computer science inventors. Hence, US must attract many diferent countries owning high technological computer inventors choose to go to US to develop their computer science profession career. Also, it seems that when many computer science inventors or professions choose to go to US to develop themselves computer science new career. In behavioral economic view, due to their leaving themselves countries choice, which may bring influence themselve country job behaviors need to be changed. They must need to adapt US new live. Because they will forgive their past computer science job. These computer science professionals need to spend time to adapt US new lives. They " past computer science job behaviors" will need to be changed to their new US any computer employer's new computer science job model.

Because their traditional computer science jobs needed to be forgot in their themselves countries. They will feel their old computer science job knowledge and behavior needed to change in order to let their US any one new of computer company employer feels satisfactory to accept their new working behavior in any one US computer organization.

So, on the other hand, many US computer company employer will feel that they must need time to accept any one new overseas computer science professions their working behaviors, their working attitude daily, because these foreign comouter science professional, their past computer working behaviors and working attitude must be different to US domestic computer science professions.

In behavioral economic view, these overseas computer science professions, their working behaviors and attitude must be needed to change in order to adapt any one US new computer company itself domestic or local computer science professional stafs themselves daily working behaviors and attitude because these overseas and local computer science professionals must need to team work together.

In behavioral economic view, it is only one way that foreign computer science professionals must need to change themselves past country traditiona daily working behaviors and attitude in order to cooperate with these US local computer science professionals in teams more easily.

Consequently, if these foreign compute science professionals can change their past working behaviors and attitude to let any one US local computer science professional feels to cooperate with them easily in short time. Then, the US computer company itself whole computer professional teams themselves efficiencies will be influenced to raised or improved by the changing past working attitude and working behaviors of these foreign computer science professionals. So, in behavioral economic view, only if US any one computer company hopes itself computer teams themselves efficiency can be raised or improved when it decides to employ foreign computer science professionals and US domestic computer science professionals. They need to work in teams together. They must need to let these foreign computer science professionals to know how to change their working behaviors and attitude to let their domestic computer science professionals feel easy to work together. Then, the US computer company itself whole team efficiency must be rasied or improved easily in short time.

● China share market investing behavior

For China share market example, economic development depends on financial market. Because if many Chinese have interest to invest to carry on shares buying and selling activities in orde to learn how to earn shares interest and share profit when the China shareholder can make decision to sell himself/herself shares in the the high price, then he/she can earn money when he/she can sell the China company's shares in the high sale share price position.

If China has many Chinese like to spend time to carry on investing shares activities. Themselves shares buying and selling behaviors will influence China has many companies can increase fund from many Chinese shareholders in order to have enough money to expand or develop themselves businesses in China in long term.

Consequently, when China can have many Chinese like to attempt to carry on buying and selling shares investing behaviors in China share market. Themselves buying and selling shares behaviors can help many Chinese companies have effort to increase enough money or capital in order to continue to do their businesses in long term absolutely. So, it explains why when many Chinese become shareholders , they can assist China will have many companies continue to develop their businesses if many Chinese like to carry on shares buying and selling investing behaviors in long time in China financial investment market nowadays in behavioral economic view.

Why has any individual country have many people invest share behavior which can influence the country's macro consumption desire?

I shall apply shares market buying and selling investment behavior to explaiin why shares investment behavior which may impact the country's overal consumption desire as below:

In behavioral economic view, I assume that when the coutry has many people have interest to attempt to carry on shares buying and selling investment behavior, then their frequent shares buying and selling behaviors which may bring negactive consumption desire or shopping desire of these shares investors their consumer behavior.

The reason is simple, when the country has many share buyers number suddenly been increasing rapidly. Consequently, these large group share investors must need to spend much time to research any kinds of company shares variations, whether when their share prices will rise up of fall down in order to achieve buying the company's shares in the lowest price and selling the company's shares in the highest price level in order to earn profit.

Basic on this reason, they must need to spend much extra time to research share prices changing behavior every day, e.g. one working person will wait to leave his/her job, after he/she can spend time to gather data to research the day's share price changing behavior after dinner. So, the working person's right time may be his/her share price market research behavior. Before he/she may spend his/her night time to go to shopping after dinner, but nowadays, he/she will fogive to do his/her shopping behavior before dinner or after dinner at hight sometime. He/she will make decision to spend much night time to turn on computer to click on share market website to research his/her share purchase choice to investigate whether his/her share price whether it rises up or falls down at the moment in order to make his/her share buying or selling decision at ever night time.

I mean the when the country has many people are share investors, their shares investment behavioral spenging time which will influence many shops lose customers at might often because the country will have many people feel need to spend night time to turn on computer or watch television to investigate share price variation. So, the country will have many people / share investors choose to stay at home in order to carry on share price variation investigation behavior, they need to listen share market update news from radios or watch the share market update news from computer or TV at home every night. Consequenly, they must reduce times to leave themselves homes at night. So, their shopping behavior also will be reduced. Because these share investors feel need to spend time to investigate share price variation news at homes which can bring economic benefits (high opportunity benefits) when they choose to forgive to leave homes to go to shopping times (opportunity cost) every night.

On conclusion, it seems that when the country has many people are share investors, then their share price investigating behavior may bring negative shopping emotion at night. Consequently, the country's any one shop may lose many customers from this share investor consumer group in behavioral economic view. Hence, when the country's share investors number had been increasing rapidly, it will influence any shops lose many customers from this share investing customer group at night frequenly in short time, even long time in behavioral economic view, because their shopping desires or shopping emotion will be brought negative feeling when they make decisions to spend much time to listen radios or watch TV or computers share price update nes at night. Hence, share market will bring negative impact to influence consumer shopping desire or negative shopping emotion in behavioral economic view.

Can technology influence human shopping behavioral change?

Nowadays, technological development has reached mature stage, whether technological mature stage may bring positive or negative shopping emotion influence to global consumers. I shall aplly internet inventin or ecommerce shopping channel tool to explain whether internet technology can bring postive or negative influence to global consumer behavior in behavioral economic view.

Internet is a good technological tool, it brings e-commerce business chance. In fact, commonly, global has have many businessmen choose to use internet channel to carry on their products transactions between global online-buyers and their electronic websites. So, global many shoppers had begun to feel online shopping is more convenient to compare visiting shops shopping. Their shopping behaviors have been changed from internet technological tool. Global has many shoppers choose to buy any products from any overseas or local businessmen their web stores. They only need to spend time to find any businessmen their webstores to choose the most suitable products to pay visa to buy from their webstores. at homes. So, in general, global had have may shoppers had changed their shopping behaviors from visiting shops to visiting webstores at homes often.

So, it seems that internet technological tool had influenced global many shops disappear, but internet webstores will be replaced their actual shops on streets. Some of businessmen either they choose webstores to replace shops or choose websotes and shops both or still keep shops only. Hence, internet tool influences global businessmen have three kinds of products sale channels to let globa local and overseas consumers to choose how to buy their products. However, in fact, many of global shoppers, youngers and olders had begun to accept to buy any products from webstores. They feel to spend time to leave homes to visit shops , their shopping behaviors will be wasted time to not essential part to their daily lives. Hence, since internet technological invention, it had changed many consumers their traditional visiting shops shopping habit to change to buying products from webstores channel.

However, on the one hand, internet creates webstores ecommerce shopping channel to let global many consumers do not need to leave homes to go to shopping. It brings negative visiting shops shopping emotion to global general consumers nowadays. But on the other hand, it also brings positive visiting internet webstores shopping emotion to global general consumer nowadays. So, it seems that global many consumers feel that they often do not need to spend much time to go out shopping. Many global consumers feel convenient and enjoy to choose any products to buy from different

internet webstores, when the online buyer chooses the most suitable product, he she only needs to pay visa card to buy the product from the online seller's webstore conveniently at home.
Hence, online shopping can bring economic benefit to online buyers, e.g. avoiding walking time or spending transport fare to visit the shop to go to shopping, shortening or reducing shopping time to do another important matter.
On conclusion, global many consumers began feel online shopping can bring more economic benefits on shortening shopping time, avoiding transport fare spending aspect. So, online shopping will be popular shopping behavior for future long time. It may encourage global many shoppers can make rapid shopping decision in short time in order to carry on any products buying transaction to global any one online shopper in short time easily in behavioral economic view. So, global many businessmen had begun to build themselves one attraction webstore in order to persuade different countries consumers to choose to click themselves webstores from internet channel to buy any kinds of products in short time easily.
So, internet technology had changed consumers traditional shopping behaviors to build positive online shopping emotion as well as raise online sellers' any products sale chance easily in behavioral economic view.

Why and how human behavior may influence the country's economic growth or recession?
When one country has many people choose to do the same matter for one period, whether their behavior may influence the country's pvera; economic growth or recession . I shall attempt to indicate cases toexplain their relationship as below:
For flowing rubblish behavioral case example, do you feel that when the country has many people often flow rubblish on the streets, instead of their flowing rubblish behavior may bring streets dirty? But, their flowing rubblish behavior may explain that this country has people may have enough money to buy food to ear, or enough cloths to wear, enough bottles of water to drink, even they may have enough money to buy new television, radio, refrigeraters , washing

machines, desktops or laptops electronic home products from old to new to use in order to satisfy their living needs. So, when they flow old electronic home products, their flowing old home electronic products behaviors may seem that they have enough money to buy other new home electronic products to replace old home electronic products to use at homes.

However, it seems thaat this country ought have many people have jobs to do. So, many of them, they can easy to make purchase decison to flow any old home electronic products and buy any new home electronic products to use . Because this country has many people have jobs to do. So, they can often not use old home electonic products to become rubblishs to flow on streets after they had bought any kinds of new home electronic homes.

In fact, it also implies that this country's economy grows rapidly. So, many businesses can glow up rapdly. When they expanded their businesses, they must need to increase employees number in order to let they help themselves to raise productivity or serve their clients absolutely. So, when the country has many businesses can grow up, it seems that its economy must be better or it is improved to compare past. Due to many different kinds of home electronic products had been often bought to use by this country people in this period. So, this country's any streets can be observed that expensive electronic home products were flowed on streets anywhere. then, this country will have many electronic home products sellers can sell their home electronic products very easily. When this country has many people can find any kinds of jobs to do easily. So, due to unemploymen rate had been decreasing.

In behavioral economic view, as this many electronic home products rubblish country case, we can observe this country may have many people have jobs to do. So, consumption number has been increased long time. So, cheap food, or expensive home electronic products may be rubblish on any streets. This country's people , their flowing rubblish behaviors may be explained that many of people have enough jobs to do, so they have ability to buy any good taste food to eat or buy any kinds of expensive electronic home products to use. So, this country's economy may be improved for this long period. So, in behavioral economic view, when this country can have many electronic home products rubblishs are flowed on anywherer in streets frequently. It seems that this country will have many people have jobs to do, so it causes they often change old home electronic products or replaced them easily, when they have enough income to spend to buy any kinds of new home electronic products to use at homes easily. Moreover, their flowing old electronic home products behaviors also indicate that this country has many people their salaries may be increased in possible from their emplyers. When this country can have many different kinds of home electornic products are sold. It means that this country's electronic home products needs or demand had been increasing, due to many people have jobs to do and income increases to excite their living of needs also improve. Consequently, this country may seem have better economic improvement. We can observe from this country's electronic home products rubblish increasing income in theis period.

On conclusion, this country ought experience economic growth at this period. So, " flowing expensive electronic home rubblish increasing number " may seem that this country's economic growth is rapidly in this period, due to many people have jobs to do as well as salaries increase in this period.

Technology how impacts human behavior changing?

Technology how influences human behavior to bring changing? For example, online share purchase and sale transaction from smart phone brings share investor can do share buying or selling transation in any where and any time conveniently, non manual driving auto vehicle, bring car owner feels comfortable and spends free time to do other matter, e.g. reading, listening mucis in himself or herself car freely. electrical energy vehicle can help car owner to reduce air polluton and it can brings the drivers do not feel drive long time in any journeys in order to avoid air pollution for environmental protection responsible car drivers in our societies.

Thus, they will drive long time in any journeys when they can drive electronic energy cars to replace oil energy cars.

However, online technology can also bring consumers can choose to stay at homes to buy any things from seller individual online webstore conveniently. Such as online technology can bring shoppers do not need to spend much time to visit shops to buy any things. They can choose any kinds of products from any online sellers individual online webstores conveniently at homes. Online technology excite busy consumers can make purchase decision easily as well as it can help online sellers sell any kinds of products from internet easily.

In behavioral economic view, technology can change human behavior to be improved, it can let human feels comfortable, more free time ro use, rapid making any decisions, such as apply smart phones to make share purchase or sale transaction decision, online shopping decision, even travelling any where decision in short time, when the traveller finds the most cheap hotel accommodation room price and air ticket price frm any travel agent online tourism webstore, then the potential travel customer can follow the online hotel accommodation price and air ticket price data to make decision when to buy the air ticket from the airline travel agent or make decision when to prebook which hotel accommodation room to go to the country to travel from online travel agent tourism webstores. So, technology can encourage global any country travelers to make anywhere to trvel rapidly. If the traveler can find the country's general hotel rooms and airline tickets prices had been decreasing more sightly. The traveler may make travel decision to choose the country to travel in short time, then he/she can prebook the country;s any hotel room and airline ticket to pay by visa fraom the country's any hotel and airline travel agent webstores., before one week, even one month or more easily. Hence, online technology can also encourage traveler individual frequent travel times to be increased, due to global travelers can find any hotel rooms and airline tickets prices from internet conveniently at homes. They do not need to spend time to visit any airline travel agent to enquire travel choice country's hotel rooms prices and airline ticket prices. They can compare global travel of countries choices ' all hotels rooms and airline agents air tickets prices to make prebook airline seat and hotel room decision before one week, one month even six months early.

On conclusion, online technology can encourage global travelers can make travelling any where and when traveling time desicions easily. It can excite tourism industry develops in long time. Also, such as electricity cars invention can encourage environment protection car owners do car purchase decision easily, because they can choose to drive electronic energy cars to replace oil energy cars in order to avoid air pollution occurs easily. So, electronic cars can increase electronic car purchasrs number, due to many of environmental protection attitude of car owners can choose to drive electricity cars to bring air cleans, even non -manual driving cars can encourage lazy driving and free time driving car owners to choose to buy non-manual (artificial intelligent) cars to drive , because they can spend much free time to read, listen music or do any matters in themselves cars, they do not need to drive cars, robotic (AI) auto driving machine is such one non-manual driver to help them to drive themselves cars confidently. So, non-manual driving cars can attract lazy and enjoying free time driving car owners to choose to buy to replace traditional manual cars to drive easily. Moreover, online share transaction can help any share investors to make share buying and selling decision in short time easily. When they can apply smart phones technological tool to carry on share buying and selling activities easily. They can observe any share rising or falling price suitation from smart phones in any where any any time easily. So, smart phone technology can help global any shareholders to make share purchase and sale transaction easily. So, technology can encourage human makes decision in short time rapidly.

How and why employees behaviors may influence economy development?

In behavioral economy view,I believe the country's any organizational employees behavior may bring indirect relationship to influence the country's long term economic development. I shall indicate past manufacture industry social development period to explain their relationship. For many countries' past business activities had belonged to manufacturing industry, such as US, UK past before 1980 year, it focused on steel manufacturing and steel manufacturing related machine products. So, US, Uk developed countries manufacturing industries may be past main country's economic income sources. I assume US , UK past had one million number different kinds of industries. They ought had about seven houndred thousand number organizational businesses were belonged to manufactured industry. They may include:

Steel manufacturing and steel related machine manufacturing, e.g. vehicle manufacturing, home appliances, e.g. washing machine, television, radio, refrigerate cooler, heater, air condition etc. different kinds of different kinds of steel -related manufacturing machine, they were manufactured from US, UK steel machine manufacturers. So, US, Uk the other three hundred thousand number industry may be general service industry, e.g. hotel service, restaurent, cinema, public transport service, tourism lesiure , wine bar, supermarket etc. different kinds of non-manufacturing industries business organizations were operated in UK, US past before 1980 year.

So, in UK, US developed countries industry development history, they ought have high percentage of businesses belonged to steel related manufacturing machine and steel products. Also, in the past before 1980 year, US, Uk business employers , they employed many workers are manufacturing workers. They needed to spend long time to work in factories. They were skillful workers, and they are trained to manufacturing cars, washing machine, television, heater, etc. even steel itself different kinds of steel related products to prepare to deliver to their shops to sell to US, Uk local or overseas clients.

So, I believe that past UK, US ought employ many employees, they belonged to skillful manufacturing workers, manufacture increasing steel machine or steel related machine number of products rapidly daily. So, if UK, US had had many of these manufacturing factories owned high skillful workers, then their manufacturing steel-related machine or steel both kinds of products number must be influenced to raise rapidly. Consequently, their steel machine manufacturing products would been exported to overseas or would been sold to local both markets , they may be influenced to raise sale number. They (these manufacturing workers) needed to be trained to know how to manufactur these different kinds of machine products in the efficient teams and they ought to be trained to raise their efficiencies in order to shorten time to manufacturing many kinds of steel related manufacturing machine or steel itself products rapidly. So , if their efficiencies and manufacturing performance was improved, these US, UK any one manufacturing worker and their teams ought achieve raising productivities significantly.

Hence, when past UK, US manufacturing industry development period, if these two countries' any manufacturing factories could have many manufacturing workers could be trained to be skillful and proficient manufacturing workers. Then, in past every day to these factories workers, they ought help their steel or steel related manufacturing employers to raise any kinds of machine or steel products number in every team. So, when past in the manufacturing industry development, US, UK could have many factories' manufacturing workers themselves steel or steel related machine products manufacturing skill could be trained to to improve to any kinds of these machine or steel manufacuring products quality as well as their products number could be influenced to raise by themselves skillful improvement significantly every day.

Then, what would be influenced to occur to past UK, US manufacturing industry period? In behavioral economic view, when these two manufacturing industry developed countries, such as UK, US , if they had many factories workers can be trained to improve their skill in order to achieve any kinds of steel or steel-related machine products quality could be improved as well as products manufacturing number could be also increased absolutely. In consequence, past UK and US both countries ought increase themselves any kinds of steel and steel related machine products number to be supplied to themselves local shops to let local clients to choose any one kind of machine manufacturing products to buy easily as well as they could also export to supply overseas any countries to buy their different kinds of steel or steel related machine products to let overseas steel or steel related manufacturing machine product buyers, they can have many of these different kinds of these steel or steel-related different kinds of manufacturing machine from UK and UK these both countries easily to compare other countries.

On conclusion, I believe that past US, and UK macro manufacturing industry income GDP would increase significantly. So, they would have good economic growth performance because when many of these manufacturing workers themselves manufacturing effort could be improved. So, it explained when employees manufacturing abilities can influence economic growth indirectly.

Robots invention whether they can help organizations to raise efficiencies or inefficiencies?

In behavioral economic view, in any organizations, when the organization hopes its worker teams can raise efficiencies , the organization may choose to increase more workers number and/or it can provide training to improve these workets themselves skills in order to raise their efficiencies. For one warehouse example, when the warehouse increases many goods , they are needed to delivered these goods from the shelves to the delivering destination locations. If this warehouse supervisors feel these workers themselves goods delivery speeds are slow, which is possible due to this warehouse's workers number is not enough. So, this warehouse supervisor ought increase workers number in order to increase their goods delivery speed in order to deliver goods from the shelves to every indicated goods delivery destination in order to let any one lorry driver can transport the right kinds of goods and ensure the accurate goods number to transport to any one client home rapidly.

However, if this warehouse supervisor planed to buy several warehouse goods delivery robots to assist these warehouse workers to find the right kinds of goods from shelves and then deliver to the right destination location in the warehouse. So, these warehouse orkers can concentrate on counting the accurate goods number and ensuring the right kinds of goods in order to prepare to let lorry drivers to transport these goods to these goods of buyers themselvers homes rapidly. Consequently, in the first step, robots can concentrate on finding th right goods from shelves and delivers them to the right goods transportation of location destination. Then, in the second step, these warehouse workers can concentrate on counting the accurate goods number and ensuring the right kinds of goods in order to prepare to put them to the lorry. Consequently, when warehouse robots and warehouse workers can cooperate to work together, the most important, robots, can deal on finding the right kinds of goods and deal on delivering the accurate number of goods of job duty as well as these warehouse workers can only concentrte on counting the right kinds of goods number in order to avoid it has none any mistake of wrong kinds of goods and inaccurate goods of delivery number to be transported to the lorry and to deliver to any one buyer's home.

So, it seems that warehouse robots ought help any one warehouse worker to raise himself efficiency and avoid goods delivery of mistake occurrence easily as well as their help to warehouse workers that can let any one goods buyer feels their goods can be delivered to their homes rapidly. Moreover, warehouse robots can also help these warehouse workers to raise efficiencies because warehouse robots can help them to shorten goods delivery time between any one shelf and any one goods delivery destination of location in the warehuse because robots may help them to find the right kinds of goods from the right shelf in the short time. So, any one worker does not need to spend long time to seek anywhere is the right shelf location for the kind of goods when the kind of goods are needed to deliver to the buyer's home from lorry. Warehouse robots can help them to do this aspect of " finding the goods from the right shelf in short time job duty". So, any one warehouse worker only needed tospend less time to do the counting of any right kind of goods number and ensuring the right kind of goods job duty. Consequently, this warehouse 's any one worker, his any one kind of goods delivery time may be reduced, because robots' assistance and they may have more confidence to avoid mistake to deliver the wrong number of goods and/or the wrong kind of goods to any one goods buyer's home.

On conclusion, it seems that warehouse robots ought may help any one warehouse worker to raise efficiency for any one team in the warehouse as well as the warehouse any one supervisor does not need to spend much time to observe any one worker individual performance for " goods delivery job duty aspect" because their goods delivery job duty that had been replaced to do by these several warehouse robots. Robots can achieve the more accurate of right kinds of goods and the right number of goods delviery job performance to compare any one of human warehouse worker themselves right kinds of goods of delivery and right number of goods of delivery job performance. So, when robots can participate to cooperate with this warehouse's any one worker to do their goods of delivery job duty in this warehouse every day. Then, robots can raies any one of supervisor individual confidence in order to let they do not need to spend time to observe any one of worker individual whose goods of delivery job performane. They can concentrate on supervising any one worker whose goods transport to lorry in the final step in order to avoid to deliver wrong goods number and / or wrong kind of goods to any one goods buyer's home every day. Consequently, this warehouse's overall teams of their delviery of goods performance many be improved by robotss' participatin to goods of delivery task as well as this warehouse's oveall teams themselves efficiencies may be influenced to raise by robots' goods of delivery task participation.

Why social behavior may influence organizational strategy needs to be changed ?

Why any organizations need to know whether nowadays social behaivor how has been changing in order to implement the kind of the most right strategy to achieve the profit aim pursue in possible. I shall indicate nowadays ecommerce or online, customer shopping behavior to explain above question concerns they ought have close relationship between social behavior and organizational strategic choice or organizational behavioral changing need.

On nowadays ecommerce business, or online shopping model, this kind of shopping model in global many young and old age consumers like to apply internet tool to choose any country sellers website stores in order to stay at home to buy any kinds of products from themselves webstores in global societies.

In fact, online shopping model had been popular for long time above to twenty years. Most of global sellers will make decision to design themselves webstores in order to attract global many online buyers to choose to buy their products from themselves webstores. So, it seems that social consumers purchase behaviors had been changed to online shopping from internet invention.

Hence, social consumers purchase behavioral changes may influence any organizations' strategies need to be changed from visiting shops purchase strategy model to online purchase strategy model, if the seller still concentrate on concentrate on considerate how to design itelf , but neglects to considerate how to design itself webstore, e.g. how to design attract product photos to put on itself webstore, how to arrange sale price information location to be putted on webstore and visa card payment location on itself webstore in order to let any one online buyer can feel very easier to buy itself any kinds of products from itself webstore. Then, its potential online buyers will be influenced to increase number when they can find this online seller itself any kinds of products photes and every kinds of product sale price information and visa card payment channel locations easily from itself webstore.

So, it implies that nowadays any one seller ought need to design one webstore to let any one online overseas and domestic consumers can have chance to click itself webstore to choose any one kind of product to buy conveniently when he/she does not hope to leave him/her home to go to shop, because nowadays social shopping behaviors had been influenced to change when internet invention, them it gives another online purchase method to replace visiting shops purchase method to global any one buyer in nowadays societies.

So, if nowadays any one seller still concentrate on how to design itself shop display in order to put any kinds of product on shelf in order to let any one visiting shop customer to find the kind of product to buy, but it neglects to change to choose to pursue another new technological shopping method, such as webstore purchase method in order to implement effective strategy to design the most right webstore as well as in order to attract global overseas and local consumers to find itself webstore easily from website and find its any one kind of product phots and sale price and visa card payment button in order to choose to buy itself any kinds of products in the short time. Consequently I believe that the seller will lose many customers from overseas and local when its other same or similar product sellers choose to design themselves webstores in order to let global any one product buyer can buy themselves any one kind of product when they can pay visa card to buy their products from them webstores conveniently when they stay at home habitly. Then, the seller will lose many global potential customers in long time.

On conclusion, in behavioral economic view, any consumer behavioral social changing, which will influence any in order to avoid customers number loses significantly . In future time, organizations need to make rapid decision in order to implement the most reasonable and the most useful strategy in order to avoid global potential customers number reduces or lose them in long time. So, social behavioral changing environment ought influence any global organizations need to decide how to change themselves strategies in order to avoid customers loses significantly in future time.

How and why human behavior may influence economic growth or recession?

May ourselves daily behaviors influence our global societial continue economic growth or recession? Do they have cause and effect close relationship between human behaviors and global economic growth or recession? I shall apply behavioral economic theory to analyze and explain whether ourselves daily behaviors and our global societial economic growth or recession which have close cause and effect relationship as below:

Every country itself economic development must depend on any business activities, otherwise, any kinds of business activities must need ourselves business activities or behaviors in order to achieve any business activities as well as achieve the country's overall economic development in macro view.

However, any country's overall business activites or behaviors which must depend on any kinds of individual businessmen, themselves employees daily working behavior or activity or performance in order to help them to attract or increase many clients number to acieve " earning profit" aim. So, it seems that any individual business, itself overall every department individual working behavior is one main factor to influence the company's overall business performance.

For agricultural fruit and meat food farming industry example, such as New Zealand is a farming main target industry country. It had had many New Zealanders were daily themselves own farming businesses for many years. Their farming businesses include growing fruit, sheep, cow, pig pork, meat etc. food sale business. If the New Zealand farmer owned a large size farming land, then he will choose either growing fruit or feeding sheeps, pigs, cows to be meat to to transport to New Zealand supermarkets to help them to sell to their farmers meet to New Zealanders in order to earn profit. Thus, if the New Zealand farmer owned large size of farming lands, then he needs to employ many farming employees (farming workers) to help him to carry on farming business daily tasks, e.g. picking up friuts, feeding pigs, cows, sheeps to eat food daily. These daily farming jobs are very important to influence this New Zealand farmer's meats or fruits sale number whether they can be easy or diffcult to sell in New Zealand supermarkets , if these farming workers can own encough farming knowledge or skill to know how to pick up fruits method and make judgement to know whether it is right time to pick up the kind of fruits from the trees , as well as know how feed this pigs, sheeps, cows to eat food in order to let they are better health. Consequently, their farming behaviors which can let these animals can provide the best taste and enough meat from these animals to let New Zealander to buy to eat from New Zealand any one supermarket. Even these New Zealand farming workers can know whether the kinds of fruits, e.g. oranges, apples, gapes etc. fruits whether they ought be picked up from the trees at the right time. Consequently, they can make judgement to decide to pick up any kinds of the best taste fruits to let any one New Zealander to buy to eat from any one supermarket in New Zealand. Otherwise, if they do not make judegement to know whether the kind of fruit ought not be picked up because they still need longer time to continue grow up to increase fruit size and better taste from the trees in order to let any one fruit buyer can feel better taste when they eat this kind of fruit later. If they can buy this kind of fruit to eat later, then this New Zealand farmer's his fruit buyers can buy the best taste of this kind of fruit to eat from an yone supermarket in New Zealand. Consequently, many New Zealand supermarkets will choose to buy any kinds of fruits from this farmer fruit supplier when they feel this farmer's fruits can provide more better taste fruits to compare other farmers' fruits.

Thus, due to New Zealand is one farming main income source country. It's any kinds of fruits and meats need to be export to overseas to sell , instead of local sale. It's GDP percent is very high to whole country 's overall income source. So, any one New Zealand farmer individual and any one farming worker individual working behavior will influence its economy whether it is influenced to grow or recession possible. Moreover, it also seems that farming workers' farming knowledge and skill will influence themselves farming daily activities to achieve the aim of the number of increase or decrease to any kinds of fruits whether they are better taste or the number of increase of decrease to any kinds of meats whether they are better taste to supply to any one New Zealand fruit or meat buyers to eat from any one New Zealand supermarket. So, it implies that any one New Zealand farming worker individual farming behavior may influence any kinds of fruits or any kinds of meat taste because they are transported to any one supermarket to sell in New Zealand.

Consequently, if New Zealans had many farmers can teach god farming knowledge and skill to let their any one farming workers know how to decide judgement to decide when it is right time to pick up any kinds of fruits from trees , or how to grow them on soil in order to let they can grow rapidly. Then, many different kinds of fruits can be provided to let any one New Zealanders can eat the best taste of fruits when their fruits are supplied to any one New Zealand supermarkets. Even, if they knew how to feed foods to pigs, cows, sheeps to eat daily. Then they can be more health and they can provide the best taste of meats to let any one New Zealanders can buy their meats from any one New Zealand supermarkets. Moreover, their fruits and meats can be transported to overseas to let any one country fruits or meats buyers can choose any kinds of New Zealand meats and fruits to buy to eat from themselves countries supermarkets. Then, many overseas fruit and meat buyers will perfer to choose New Zealand any kinds of fruits or meats to buy to compare other countries fruits or meats to buy when they go to any one local supermarkets.

On conclusion, it seems that New Zealand farming workers themselves farming behavior may influence their farming employers any kinds of fruits or meats sale number and income because their farming task behaviors must influence whether their fruits or meats taste are the better taste or worse taste to compare their other local farmers (the farmer competitors) whose fruits or meats taste. If tthe farmer's any one farming worker can be trained to learn how to know to feed animals skill and when is the most right time to pick up any kinds of fruits from trees or how to grow them on the soil methods. Due to these farming worker individual farming behavior may influence his different finds of fruits and meats sale number to be increase or decrease, so these any one New Zealand farmer must need to depend on any one farming worker whose farming working methods, if their farming working behaviors can be the best to influence any kinds of fruits to grow rapid or any kinds of pigs, cows, sheeps animals grow up rapidly , then their sale number may be increase significantly and their taste can be improved to let any New Zealand or overseas meat or fruit buyer to buy to eat to feel from any one New Zealand or overseas supermarkets, then New Zealand's agriculture industry must be influenced to increase. In the world, any one fruit or meat buyer must choose to buy New Zealand's fruit and meat to eat in prefer to compare other countries' fruits and meats. So, New Zealand's GDP may be influenced to raise from any one New Zealand farming worker individual farming working behaviors.

Reasons why human behavior may influence economic recession or growth?

Can ourselves daily behaviors or activies influence ourselves countries' economic growth or recession? I shall attempt to explain the reasons why they have direct or indirect relationship between human behavior and economy growth or recession as below:

I shall indicate environment pollution case to attempt to explain above question. Our societies had been experiencing servious environment pollution challenge. However, environment pollution , such as air pollution is caused by air planes and vehicles emission by air planes and vehicles emission as well as water pollution is caused by plastic rubblish, or dirty water or oil or gas chemical material, these both kinds of pollution ought may bring economic recession and this both kinds of pollution are caused by human ourselves daily foolish activities.

I believe human behavior and economy and pollution which have cause and effect relationship. I shall analyze this environment pollution case to explain why they have case and effect relationship between human foolish behavior and environment pollution and economic recession as below:

When global societies had many people like to buy cars to drive to bring emission to fresh air on the roads as well as many manufacturing factories will bring emission to pollute fresh air in their manufacturing processes. Factories and cars will bring air pollution , due to factories need to pollute fresh air in order to manufacture many products and car owners need to drive their cars to go to offices or leisure places. Their cars will also bring emisson to pollute fresh air. On consequence, car owners themselves frequent driving behaviors and factory workers themselves frequent manufacturing behaviors may bring environment pollution. Technology or human behavior whether may influence economic growth or recession. Moreover, air planes also brings emission to pollute air when they are flying in sky. Also, when ships bring oil pollution or sea plastic rubblishs bring pollution to global oceans.

In fact, manufactuers and cars owners, such as factories workers manufacturing behaviours ans car owners driving behaviors and pilots driving air planes flying behaviors and ships transport behaviors, which may cause plastic rubblish, oil or gas emission to sky or sea or on the road to cause ocean and air pollution is serious. However, human ourselves need to buy cars to drive to satisfy ourselves driving leisure or enjoyment, travelers need to catch air planes to travel to enjoy leisure needs, factories workers need help factories to manufacture many products to sell to customers to satisfy their using needs. oil exploration needs to find lands to explore new oil lands.

All of these business and leisure activites may bring serious air and water pollution. However, due to serious air and water pollution will bring earth warming challenge , such as some countries temperature will be influences to rise up to 40 degree or higher br earth warming. However, earth warming is caused by air and ocean pollution. Pollution must be caused by human ourselves, driving cars leisure and factories manufacturing business activities. Hence, if human decided to continue to do these foolish behaviors, we only pursue to manufacture different kinds of industrial products or drive cars to enjoy leisure aims, but we also neglect ourselves behaviors may bring environment pollution. Then, earth warming or earth temperature will be influenced to rise up absolutely in long term. Moreover, if our future earth will be influenced to bring serious high temperature effect by human ourselves these foolish behaviors.

On consequencey, warth warming will bring serious economic losses in possible because when ourselves earth temperature had been influenced to rise up to 40 degree or high. Ourselves health will be caused poor, duc to we will feel difficult breath, we must need often tried and hard to work, due to our nervous and health will be influenced to poor by pollution and earth warming effect. Also, we need to pay more money to see doctors when we had long life. Then, our societies will lose may strong labors to help manufacturers to work, e.g. factories will reduce workers number to help manufacturers to produce more different kinds of products, due to workers health is general poor. Due to lacking enough workers to manufacture products, our societies will begin to reduce enough supply number of products to sell to global consumers to satisfy their use needs.

On conclusion, in behaviroal economic view, our societies will lose many labors due to their bodies are not health by air and water pollution. Global economic and business activities will be influenced to worse by global workers reducing number reason. So, economic recession will begin to occur in possible when pollution reaches the serious level.

How employee behavior influences organizational development?

Can any organizational department employee individual behavior may help the organization to bring long term development? When one employee individual behavior, manager won't feel whose task behavior may help organizational development, but when the department has many teams cooperate to work together , all of these team employees whose task behaviors may help their organization to bring long term development.

I shall explain how any why when the organization has many departments, as well as when every team memmber individual behavior may help whole organization to bring long term development in possible as below:

Every organization must need efficient department to cooperate to work together. They may include human resource, finance, logistic, facility management, sales, marketing , operateional , warehouse , factory manufacture , research and development, purchase, customer service etc. different kinds of departments to cooperate to work together. So, any one employee individual behavior, include manager, leader, supervisor, worker, salesperson, manufacture worker, adminisration staff, factory or logistic worker etc. themselves task behavior whether his/her performance is worse or better , whose task behavior ought bring long term good or bad influence to cause the organization's whose efficiency, or performance , whether it can be influenced to improve significantly. For car factory manufacture workers department example, it exmploys 100 car manufacturing workers. They need to manufacture at least 50 cars in order to bring enough car manufacture number to supply to global car buyers to choose to buy (satisfaction to car buyers their driving leisure activity needs). However, if this car manufacture firm employs many low skilful car manufacture workers, their inefficient car skill may bring cars manufacture number reduces, they can not achieve to reach the at least 50 cars manufacture number, if these 100 car manufacture workers. They have half number of workers, they only manufacture 30 to 40 cars number at least daily. So, it seems that this car manufacture firm will have half car manufacture workers bring the low cars manufacture number to compare the another half cars manufacture workers, when this proficient car manufacture workers may manufacture at least 60 or more cars manufacture number daily. So, it explains that this inefficient car manufacture workers will not help this car manufacture company to manufacture enough cars number in order to supply to global car market to sell to satisfy global car buyers needs, when car buyers demand number is more thn car manufacture supply number in supply and demand view. Hence, in long term, if this car manufacture company can not employ new proficient car manufacture workers to replace those inefficient or low skillful car workers. Consequently, its car manufacture number must be influenced to reduce and it can not satisfy global car buyers driving leisure needs.

However, if this car manufacture firm also has shop to sell itself any kinds of cars, instead of manufacturing cars product. So, it needs have both main departments to help it to earn profit. The first step, it needs have proficient car manufacture workers to help it to manufacture at least 50 cars from every car worker in order to have enough cars number to be provided to global car sellers to help it to sell to global car customers. Second step, if it decided to attempt to sell itself cars. Then, it needs to set up car shops in global to different countries in order to let global car buyers may visit its global any one car shop to enquire any one car etc. salesperson about any car quality, speed, gas useful, price, safety, etc. information questions and they can attempt to sit in any one car to feel whether which car can let them to feel more comfortable to make final car purchase decision in any one shop. So, if this car company can provide good sale speaking skillful training to any one car salesperson to let his/her to know whether how to explain every kind of car function and feature, manufacture method etc. questions, then I believe that they can influence any one car buyer to makecar purchase choice decision more easily. So, it this car manufacturer hopes it may attempt to earn profit from different countries car sellers and car buyers both. It ought also provide training course to all general car salespeople to be proficient owning sale speaking skillful professional skill in order to prepare having more confidence to persuade any one car customer to make car purchase choice from any one car salesperson more easily to compare global other car sellers.

Hence, if this car manufacturer could build both car manufacturing team and car sale team more proficient. However, if this car manufacturer hopes to develop itself car manufacture busness to expend to car sale business both in success. It must need to spend long term to provide training courses to general car manufacture workers and general car salespeople both to be proficient car skillful manufacture workers and proficient car skillful salespeople in order to help they can manufacture enough car numbers and help they can persuade may car customers can make car purchase decision in short time when they visit its any one car shop.

However, this car manufacture company explains why every car manufacture worker whose manufacturing behavior and every car salesperson sale persuading speaking ability may help this car manufacture company to expand from its car manufacture market to car sale market development in sussess in possible. So, this car manufacture firm must need these two kinds of essential human resource elements in order to achieve its cars sale number and cars manufacture number increasing aim. They may include proficient car manufacture workers and proficient car salespeople both human resource elements. These both human resource daily task behavior may influence its long term task efficient performance in order to expand itself car sale business in success from itself car manufacture business easily. If it hopes to expand its car manufacture business to car sale business in success. It must need to provide training to these two departments general staffs to be proficient staffs in order to supply enough cars number to its global car shops to let global car buyers can choose its any kinds of cars to buy in any time.

Morevoer, if this car manufacture company can have good skillful of car research and development department , it aims to research and innovate any new technological cars invention in order to improve its any traditional old kinds of cars to be innovative new kinds of cars from every year. Consequently, its any new innovative cars ought attract global any one car buyer to make car purchase choice final decision more easily, because its any kinds of manufacturng cars can be innovated rapidly to compare its any one car manufacturing competitors, when its nay kinds of cars can be shorten time to innovate within three months, but its any one car manufacturing competitors need to spend more than three months, even one year to innovate themselves traditional old cars products in long term.

Hence, its car staffs research and development department staffs must need own good car product design ability, proficient car engineering knowledge , even car invention knowledge in order to innovate its any one kind of car product in short time and introduce to let its global car proficient car buyers feel surprise to its any one kind of innovativc car products to compare its any one car manufacturer.Hence, these four departments: car manufacture, car sale and car research and development anr car training departments must need concentrate resource to provide enough training to any one staffs in order to achieve the best performance.

On conclusion, all these departments staffs their performance can influence car manufacture aim to chance to car manufacture and sale aim more significantly. it explains why some main department staffs whole behaviors may influence any organizational performance significantly.

CHAPTER TWO

How social chance influences Disney visitor leisure need change

Apply knowledge management method to predict Walt Disney entertainment theme park behavioral consumption

Disney organizational structure knowledge management strategy changing (Internal weaknesses changes to internal strengths)

Walt Disney entertainment thems park had ever applied psychological methods to find what factors had caused its visitor numbers to be decreased. As Harriet Griffey (2010) stated that "sometimes, boredom can give disadvantages to reduce staffs' ability to motive to work and reduces positive emotion , such as happiness. Thus, it causes people (staffs) lack motivated reasoning to unconsciously evaluate evidence in ways consistent with whose preferences. This type of bias can hinder a company's ability to learn from mistakes and to build successful strategies."

However, Disney needed to implement knowledge management strategy to satisfy visitors demand after who entered .Disney demanded cleaners to repeat to remember any information to prepare to answer visitors' enquiries. It will train every cleaner memory to remember any information to be long term from short term memory successfully and every cleaner won't feel bore to do only cleaning job duty. When every one feel places are clean, who will concentrate on answering any visitors enquiries as the same time. Even, if they can give excellent service performance to serve visitors to let who to know how to go to any places in the short time. It is possible that visitors will appreciate whose service performance to let their manager to know, so that every cleaner will have chance to raise salary. Besides, waiting time and queues are daily problem for Disney theme park. Fast lines or priority queues appear as a solution of efficient queues for clients. Disney understood fast ticket line system affected visitor attendance numbers. Disney entertainment facilities long waits leaded to lower service evaluations and greater customer dissatisfaction. Efficient queue waiting time management can improve Disney visitor satisfaction and the willingness to recommend the service. Disney analysed of theme park visitor behaviour in relation to pay the higher ticket price to select to pay more for fast queuing line ticket than common queuing line ticket. In fact, Disney fast queuing line ticket system choice gave potential queues to any waiting clients . In general, Disney visitors don't like to wait long time in every entertainment facilities queuing line, who will feel a waste of time and waiting can lead to negative emotional response like frustration, impotence, tension or irritation .

In fact, Disney amusement theme park needed visitors wait long queues and delays which were a frequent occurrence in every entertainment facilities line. Disney theme park as sets of rides, spectacles and leisure mechanisms are intended to entertainment and spark the imagination of clients, allowing visitors to escape their daily routing. In result, waiting is often a problematic issue that can influence Disney visitor experience and that can appear as one of the principal motives for complaining. As Disney visitor demand fluctuates constantly and demand patterns are often difficult to predict. It caused extra staff needed for the extra line. Finally, priority services such as fast line system facilities segmentation of its amusement park. When Disney offer the possibility of purchases a fast line, which are creating two different group. Disney visitors who are highly sensitive to waiting times are willing to pay to avoid or reduce lines or visitors that are highly sensitive to price that prefer to wait rather than to pay extra money. Also, Disney provides extensive training opportunity for participants through its own Disney university. The question of whether their training opportunity can lead the improve human resource activities. On the third hand problem, Disney are also worried that employees may leave it and join other competitor to serve their parks after training. Disney shows a trend of increasing depending on human capital other than physical capital. It thinks human capital is the knowledge, skills, ideas and commitment of its employees. It explains that investing in training and development is essential to its client service growth. In fact, Disney had owned enough entertainment facilities, restaurants, hotels, shopping centres within theme park, but its visitor numbers are increasing to need to be served satisfactorily. However, it needs to train cleaners, entertainment facilities service staffs, queuing service staffs, hotels, restaurants, shopping centres service staffs, instead of it's entertainment facilities attraction.

Disney observes that spending on training and development is typically regarded as consumption, instead of investment. On job training usually can't be replaced by formal education, therefore Disney chooses to make contribution on providing further training and development to employees. Disney paid salary for staff training, which included classroom, seminars, symposia or conferences; computer based training, on site training, book and periodicals reading, formal mentoring and informal mentoring program opportunities to meet its old staffs and new staffs both needs of motivate factors to achieve advancement , achievement, personal growth responsibility and achievement and recognition to raise its business performance effectively and efficiently.

However, Disney's amount of training has a positive influence on intrinsic motivation of its employees. Job satisfaction, salary, working condition, its policies, administration, relationship with supervisors, peers and subordinates are Disney factors to influence it's human resource activities performance. Disney training contents include these functional area: Raising excellent service performance include that hotel food and beverage service delivery, shopping center, merchandise sale, restaurant service, entertainment facilities queuing waiting service, cleaning and enquiring how to go different locations in Disney, cashier service etc. They are very important to influence visitor numbers. Disney implementation of knowledge management solution to improve queuing waiting line process. The use of Disney front line service staffs as human capital combined with knowledge of customer preference has made the fast pass an innovation solution to enhance queuing in the Disney theme parks.

Disney ability to capture customers in virtual queues when giving them a pleasurable waiting experience has made them a leader in knowledge management initiatives in the service industry. Disney's emphasis on human capital within their theme parks, combined with traditional queuing theory to create more pleasurable waiting environments. Hence, Disney showed the value of tacit employee knowledge integrated with traditional queuing theory to reduce loss of customer satisfaction to enhance, goodwill and profitability. Knowledge management expresses itself as human action in form of evaluation, attitudes, points of view, commitments, motivation etc. It seemed that Disney agreed that human capital (people, knowledge, ideas, creativity) maybe today's most valuable commodity.

Knowledge Management Strategy was used to queue control from Disney. Disney managers have long understand the pressure of waiting time and revenue; who know that every minutes spent

waiting in queuing is a minute that the client is not generating revenue. So, Disney managers have processed with design of a reservation system recognizes that guests can be freed from physically standing in the actually and perception of waiting by allowing guests to engage has arrived. Cope et al., (2008) showed that" the system was first tested at Disney in 1998. Managers assessed the system by surveying guests who used it. Results were positive and indicated that guests spent substantially less time in queuing, spent more per capita, and saw significantly more attractions, satisfaction level sky rocketed.The system was expanded in 1999 to include five of the most popular park attractions and was named FASTPASS. The system has since been expanded to all Disney theme parks worldwide, and is now in use by over 50 million guests per year .That guests have two options .Namely, they can choose to Obtain a FASTPASS ticket and come back a later, designed time or Wait in a traditional queuing. Guests are assisted in making their choice by information regarding estimated waits of both options. Thus, can decide to wait in the traditional queuing, or take a FASTPASS ticket and return it a later time with no further wait. Once an assigned FASTPASS time is generated and provided to a guest, it is valid for the 60 minutes beyond that time, creating a window in which guest can return."
There are numerous benefits in allowing park guests to return to an attraction within a designed time frame. Queue Waits involve managing two major client issues:

1.How long Disney visitors actually wait every time queue.
2.How long Disney visitor think they are waiting by whose psychological feeling every time queue.

Thus, if they feel that who spend much time to queue, it will cause they feel angry and they also feel admission ticket price is paid too high to them unfairly. In general, clients were allowed the ability to see two attractions during the time they would have previously been able to see only one. This can viewed as an implementation of a multi-phased system, depending on the attraction picked, each queuing may be single channel attractions, the guest creates whose own multi phase system. Obvious, results, were that guests were able to engage in more revenue producing activities, saw more of the popular attractions and began to par take care, in other less utilized attractions .

Wiig defined(1993)" Knowledge management in different ways and from different perspective. The emphasis is on human know how and how it brings value to an organization. Intangible asset contributes to corporation objective may be immeasurable and isn't simple to evaluate the impacts of knowledge management." However, Knowledge management may not be only factor influencing organizational performance. In fact, Disney refined technology utilization to improve the user design of all human resource related systems, improving timeliness (queue waiting time deduction), setting elapsed time goals and monitor performance towards those standards, considering to use of automated fast queue waiting system, evaluating staffing levels, a close examination of adequacy of current staff level is warranted, beyond to improve visitors satisfaction. Clients holding fast pass tickets may choose to visit a gift shop or any park concessions. Thus, Disney has ability to co-branded products and service. Disney's approach combining queuing and human capital.

Dunn, J et al., (2002) showed "The use of fast pass provides an insightful application of the combination of techniques of queuing and human capital to strategically leverage knowledge management principle .When waiting lines are an part of the Disney experience, park guests build magical memories through innovation. It is Disney's recognition of front line service staffs that transforms that employees into knowledge who multi task in their roles.For example, an attraction host or a street sweeper may be a valuable Source knowledge to park guests. In addition to their primary roles, they may have a wealth of information about attractions for guests. They may be able to give directions, provide schedules, and offer helpful suggestions from their daily observation. This is the first stop to increase knowledge management . Next, Disney improves its clients' perception by minimizing the perception of waits. The use of the fast pass enables Disney not only to enhance the psychological aspect of waiting lines, but also to capitalize at the same time." Instead, Disney needed to give people specific tools designed to help them to do their job and solve specific business problems. Thus, after Disney learned how it applied the knowledge management method to solve its challenges, e.g. Human capital and queuing theory provide two very different valuable assets to raise its competitive abililty. Then, its visitor numbers was increasing largely and quickly.

It seems Disney understand what which visitor's individual psychological needs, who needs to pay reasonable ticket fee and who also dislike to need to wait long time to queue to play any entertainment facilities. Disney also understand cleaners have extra time to serve visitors when who can answer any visitor individual enquiries immediately. After the cleaners will feel satisfactory and happy if who can give positive feedback from any visitor individual enquiry. The cleaner will feel more valuable to Disney employer, due to who can do any enquiry duty during whose working hours. The most important, who have chance to get higher salary and promotion. Thus, Disney can predict visitor and staff individual psychological needs, then it can raise new and keep old visitor numbers and keep old staffs to choose to stay to it's organization to work for long term. It can earn more economic benefit for long term after it can predict whose staffs and visitors whose psycholgical needs successfully.

1.2 Disney market research method (global macro economic theme park player marker research)

In macro behavioral economy view point, it can explain why market research can predict consumption behavior for Disney consumers. Disney can use market research method to predict what consumer behavior trend. In general, consumer will have choice behavior, when who needs to do decision to buy automobile among of more than one product choice or with the determinants of such consumer behavior as buying life insurance, putting money in a pension plan, using credit cards etc. actions.

By comparison, questions about behaviors that involve a choice among less or more options are usually studied at a lower level of generality. Thus, consumption psychologists may be interested to know why consumers buy one second of automobile rather than another, why who choose one type of medical treatment over another, or why who fly one airline rather than another. So, consumption psychologists must clearly define the action, target, context and time elements of the behavioral alternatives to predict whose consumption behavior. For example, the decision to buy tickets on one airlines rather than another can be affected by the destination (target element): A consumer may prefer one airline for overseas flights , but another for domestic flights. Similarly , choice of insurance company may vary depending on whether who buy life insurance, automobile insurance or property insurance.

Why will decisions under uncertainty cause? In consumer choice process, who has chance to encounter decisions under uncertainty. For example, the attributes of each product were assumed to be known with certainty. Thus, the consumers knew the price, picture, quality, reliability and visual appeal of each product type. All consumers need to do was to be importance weights and subjective values to these attributes and then derive a weighted average. In many of choice alternatives are not known with certainty ahead of time. Often, the outcomes are produced by decision depend on the state of the world at the time and the decision is made. For another example, a LCD television can produce a high -definition picture only of the service providers transmit high-definition programs. To take this uncertainty into account, the consumer has to judge not only the value of a high-definition display , but also the likelihood that this attribution will be available.

Perhaps, more readily recognized are the risks and uncertainties inherent in investment decisions. The investment outcomes of a decision to invest in a fixed interest certificate of deposit or a stock market mutual fund depend on future market conditions. Whereas the CD produces a known payoff over a given time period, the amount and probability of possible gains or losses to be expected of the mutual fund can only be estimated.

Thus, advertising can reduce decision uncertainty to consumers' choices. If the product advertising can attract to consumer's consideration , it will persuade the consumer to choose to buy the brand of product. Clearly, information about the decision making process, in general, as well as about decisions of particular relevance to consumer behavior. Thus, it seems advertising information can reduce consumers' choices processes under uncertainty to decide to buy the brand of product preference choice.

Why businessmen need to divide customer segment(s) to decide who is target customer group to predict consumer behavior. Nowadays, consumers are unique in themselves. A comprehensive knowledge of consumers and their consumption behavior is essential for a firm to succeed. In order to understand and predict consumption patterns and behaviors within segment(s), market research becomes essential.

Why businessmen need to concern market research with consumer behavior (global macro economy marker research). Each individual is unique himself/herself and needs and wants vary from person to person. Markets identify segments and target one or few of these segments and target one or few of these segments and thereby fulfil the qualifications of the marketing concept. First, marketers need to identify customer needs and wants and then, deliver product and service offering, so as to satisfy the customers more efficiently and effectively, than the competitors.

In macro behavioral economic marketing research method view

point, Such as Disney, in order to understand and predict each visitor consumption pattern and behavior within segment(s), e.g. young, adult, old age, rich and poor segment. It seems Disney has many different age , student or working people customer segments. So, market research becomes essential to assist Disney to predict what different market segment needs. Such as young age segment needs excitement, e.g. entertainment facilities to play . Otherwise, old age segment needs not excitement entertainement facilities , this old age segment needs to walk in Disney garden or go to shopping centre or sit down to watch Disney movies etc. not excitement activites to. Market research defines to gather information about market and the customers. The environment of a firm, such as Disney may be grouped as the micro and macro environment both. The micro environment firm comprises forces to close affect the firm directly. For example, the firm's internal environment, the founder/leader and whose vision and mission, clients, competitors, suppliers and channel intermediaries.

The macro environment, on the other hand, companies forces in the environment that first affect the micro environment and thought that which affect the firm, in other words, which affect the firm indirectly, including the demographic factors, socio-economic factors, political factors, technological factors, cultural factors, natural factors etc. The micro environment is studied in terms of strength(s) and weakness and when the macro environment is studied in terms of opportunities and threat(s) analysis of both comprises the SWOT analysis.

Thus, Disney market research can help which to understand the specific marketing situation facing . Identifies the needs and wants of Disney different age client segment(s), identifies variables age target segment(s), serves them better through formulation of appropriate marketing strategies a mix of the 4(p)s. It's goal is to achieve maximum efficiency and effectiveness to meet customer needs and wants and client satisfaction . Thus is obtained through a conscious attempt at understanding " what" the disney young or old age target needs, "why" who needs, "when" who needs, from "where" who needs, "how" much who needs and "how" often who needs during who are staying in Disney theme park at the staying time. Thus, the integration of Disney market research with Disney visitors behavior: Disney marketing research can understand and predict any different age segment behavior as well as Disney consumer research is a process and tools to be used to study what consumer behavior is or who expect to buy when Disney visitors are staying in Disney theme park.

Marketing research objective is to study the marketing environment and the clients who are a part of it, as well as to study consumers as individuals as groups. It focuses to establish trends and identify opportunities and threats in the environment, to study the market and forecast potential and to predict buying patterns based on modeling and , to understand consumption behavior and consumption patterns. Besides, consumer behavior research has tradition approach and current approach has traditional approach and current approach.

Traditional approach divides positivist and interpretivist both approaches. Positivist approach refers to as modernism is the earliest approach to studying consumer behavior and trends the study as an applied science. It lays emphasis on the causes of consumer behavior, these causes are directly related to effects. Thus it treats consumer as "rational" human things, who make purchase decisions after collecting information and weighing all alternatives. The process of consumer decision making, it seems of rationality, rational decision making and problem solving is the key. It is based on certain assumption, consumer actions based on cause and effect relationship can be generalized, who can be objectively measured and tested. If researchers could identify the reasons behind consumption behavior, who would be able to predict it, and if who could predict consumer behavior, who could influence it.

The methods focus on prediction of client behavior, including surveys, observations and experiments. It aims at drawing conclusions a large samples. The positivist consumer actions can be objectively measured and tested. It focuses to predict consumer behavior, e.g. large samples of quantitative methodology. Otherwise, the interpretivist consumer action is a cause and effect relationship can't be generalized , consumption pattern and behaviors are unique, these are unpredictable. Consumer actions are unique and different both between two consumers, and/or within the same consumer at different times and situations. It can't be objectively measured, tested and generalized. It focuses the act of understanding the consumption rather than predicting the act of purchase, e.g. methodology small samples of qualitative methodology.

In consumption psychological view point, the current approach is the term " dialectics" , considers all forms of human behavior, thus the current approach to the study of consumer divided into four approaches: materialism approach implies that consumer behavior is shaped by the material environment, e.g. money, possessions etc. , change approach means consumer behavior is " dynamic" in nature, it is always in a process of continuous motion, transformation and change. Totality means consumption behavior is " interconnected" with other forms of human contradiction means views changes in consumer behavior as arising from their internal contradictions, like moods, emoting etc. The approach studies the consumer as a complex total whole and views consumer purchase as well as consumption processes.

The current approach to studying consumer behavior uses both the quantitative as well as qualitative approaches. There are three broad research perspectives in consumer behavior: they are as follows:

Decision making perspective, the experiment perspective and behavioral influence perspective. According to decision making perspective , the buying process is a sequential in nature, with the consumer perceiving that there exists a problem and that moving across a series of logical and rational steps to solve the problem; stages being problem recognition, information search, evaluation of alternatives , purchase decision and past purchase behavior, it emphasizes rational , logical and cognitive approach to consumer decision making and purchase process.

The experiential perspective believes that not all buying may be rational and logical, in some cases, buying results are from a consumers' desire for fun and fantasy, pleasures, emotions and moods. The perspective emphasizes that consumers are feelers as well as thinkers. The behavioral influence perspective holds that forces in the environment stimulate a consumer to make purchases without developing beliefs and attitudes about the product.

In general, quantitative research is used by the positivists and qualitative research is used by interpretivists. How to use quantitative research in consumer behavior? It comprises (i) research techniques that are used to gather quantitative data over large samples randomly and (ii) statistical tools and techniques, e.g. survey, observation and experiments techniques. Thus type of research is descriptive in nature. It is primarily used by the positivists when studying consumer behavior with a focus on prediction of consumer behavior and techniques are also used by " dialectics" approach.

How to use qualitative research in consumer behavior? It comprises (i) research techniques that are used to gather quantitative data over small samples techniques , e.g. depth interviews, focus group of study is subjective in nature. The focus is on understanding consumption behavior and consumption pattern . the objective is to gain an understanding of consumer behavior and the causes marketing situations are unique, and hence the finding can't be generalized to marketing situations. It is primarily used by the interpretivists when studying consumer behavior. However, the qualitative techniques are also used by " dialectics" approach.

Today, both approaches and are used to study consumer behavior. In some causes, qualitative research may act as an indicator to qualitative research through case studies and other qualitative measures. Qualitative research is very often a prelude to quantitative research are used to prepares scales for surveys and experiments. So, macro economic marketing research method is situation to Disney entertainment theme park to predict entertainment theme park consumer's psychology.

1.3 Disney entertainment theme park consumer psychological method: Brand image attention of behavioral consumption of prediction method

Brand is one good behavioral economy method to persuade Disney consumption. Disney can apply brand image prediction method to attract visitors visiting choice. Disney is one famous entertainment theme park in the World. The application of disney visitor consumption psychology, and in particular to Disney branding, has gained popularity over the past decade in academic research and business practice. What neuroscience can bring to advance Disney entertainment theme park understanding of the consumer psychology of brands choice of behavioral consumption. The Disney brand preference formation over time has four basic components: (1) representation and attention, (2) predicted value , (3) experienced value and (4) remembers value and learning.

First, on representation and attention component, it means that the amount of information consumers are exposed to is enormous, yet consumer's processing capacity is limited. How Disney consumers represent, attend to, and perceive incoming information may have a profound influence on their behavioral consumption , i.e. Disney brand identification. Representation is the first process in entertainment theme park industry brand decisions , which involves forming the representation of the choice alternatives, that is brand identification. For example, different beer brands provide different options for choice are identified to consumers. At the same time, the entertainment theme park consumer needs to integrate information on internal state , (e.g. thirst level) and external states , e.g. (location , social context) that drive attention. For example, when faced with a choice between a entertainment theme park consumer's choice is likely to depend on whose own level of entertainment theme park playing facilities (an internal state) and level of entertainment facilities chooses to play (an external state). However, the entertainment theme park brand image is a visual system allows for rapid entertainment theme park brand and entertainment service performance identification. One of the key questions at this stage is what entertainment theme park consumers pay attention to (i.e. focus on) once who are exposed to a number of rapidly identified entertainment theme park choice alternatives (i.e. theme park images).

Attention is the mechanism responsible for selecting the information that gains preferential status above other available information for researching on entertainment theme park image. Thus, if the entetainment theme park brand image is attractive, then it will be probable attract the initial eye movement of entertainment theme park consumers and thus may have a profound effect on related theme park consumer behavior.

For example, Pieters and Wedel (2007) showed that ensuring that consumers pay attention to the brand displayed in a print ad. It is the most effective way to ensure that who will transfer their attention to other elements of the print ad. So, entertainment theme park image of attractive visual selection and eye movement can enhance the quality of incoming information to consumer individual behavioral consumption for the entertainment theme park of choice. The suggestion of eye-tracking is as a useful tool for determining the extent to which entertainment theme park consumers find different entertainment facilities images extensions plausible. In sum, representation and attention are complex processes that influence all subsequent steps in our brand decisions framework.

Next, the step is predicted value, it is of each (entetainment theme park image) brand that is available for choice to represent the entertainment theme park consumer's belief about the experienced value of that brand at same time in the future. In other words, the predicted values involves the consumer's evaluation of how much enjoyment who will desire form playing theme park facilities among of different theme park of entertainment service choice. For example, clothes are at different retail stores (e.g. H&M vs. Zara), consumer who are loyal to a store as measured by real purchasing behavior. (i.e. amount spent, frequency and recent of purchases based on loyalty card data) show more activation in the compared to consumers who are less loyal. The cloth brand inviting loyalty card holders who will be persuaded by the brand . So, the loyalty card of the brand, e.g. Disney loyalty card of park's visitors can be the predicted value to the Disney image of the entertainment facilities to persuade the Disney loyalty card holders to choose to pay admission fee to enter Disney theme park to play.

Next, the step is experienced value , it is based on the pleasure derived from consuming a brand, such as Disney entetainment facilities service. It is a concept of motivational value to the consumer. Motivational value is a concept that is related to how predicted and experienced values interact is the motivational value or incentive of an option to the consumer. So building good brand image memory us important to influence consumer psychology. For example, the information of channel ,.e.g. ad. can build brand image memory to consumer more easily. Thus, good brand image can build good memory to consumers to prefer to choose to buy the brand of product easily. Otherwise, bad brand image can build bad memory to consumers to not prefer to choose to buy the brand of product easily. Thus, manufacturers or sellers can not neglect how to build good brand image to attract any consumer individual attention by attrative advertising because good brand image has close relationship with psychological consumption for shopping. It seems brand loyalty of famous degree can help businessmen to predict whether consumers are accepting or are not accepting to choose to buy their products or consume their service provision more accurate. For example, if the product brand is very famous long term, it seems consumers are accepting to choose to buy the product. Otherwise, if the product brand is not famous long term, it seems consumers are not ccepting to choose to buy the product.

1.4 Consumer psychological method:

Can scientific research method predict Disney visitors behavior ?

Using scientific research methods to predict Disney consumption behavior phenomena in this field, some experts had attempted to do research in predictive validity to evaluate whether a measure of scientific achievement to consumer behavior. There are three groups thought to have varying knowledge of and ability to predict consumer behavior are academics, marketing practitioners and consumers in general. Academic groups use their scientific knowledge of consumer behavior as a basic for such activities as teaching, consulting for corporations, and testifying in legal and regulatory proceedings.

In contrast, marketing practitioners are likely to be as familiar with this scientific literature. However, practitioners gain expertise through their experience. This expertise might help them to make accurate predictions of consumer behavior. Finally, when few studies on consumer behavior reach the general public, consumer's personal experiences should help them to predict certain aspects of customer behavior. So, it seems that whether Disney ought choose to do consumer behavioral psychological method to predict consumer behavior, such as personal experiences (psychological feeling) method is more accurate than to scientific method, such as marketing research method.

In this discussion, I shall imply two hypotheses about why Disney experts ought measure consumer behavior by behavioral psychological method predictions more than scientistic method, such as marketing research method .

The first hypothesis, experts can make more accurate predictions than novices as well as the second hypothesis, academics can make more accurate predictions them practitioners. Thus, these hypotheses bring the questions and asked the subjects to predict whether each hypothesis tended to be true or false. For example, whether the more frequently an adolescent interacts with peers about consumption matters is the greater the tendency to use peer preferences in evaluating products? (Moschis & Moore, 1979).

Will a person be more satisfied with their recently purchased car if the car met or exceeded whose expectations? (Westbrook 1980).

Hence, using behavioral psychological prediction method , it will ask these these questions to gather the data to attempt to analyze what factors can influence whose satisfied feeling during who play any Disney entertainment facilties. These survey questions can include: Will a disney visitor feel more satisfied to play any Disney entertainment facilities with who recently visited Disney if the Disney entertainment facilities met or exceed whose expectation? Whether the more frequently Disney entertainment facilities a player with whose friends who have more satisfied feeling to play any Disney entertainment facilities to compare the less frequently Disney entertainment facilities another player alone or no any friend?

A long term survey research indicated that a consumer reserch result for the practitioner group, who worked with marketing problems, but who were unlikely to be familiar with scientific research on consumer behavior. For example, systematic sampling was used to select 100 practitioners from the 1984 year American Marketing Assocication Membership Directory (academic addresses were excluded), a self addresses envelope was enclosed in the original mailings, and two postcard reminders were sent. Replies were received from 20 academics and 13 practitioners.

Subjects were asked whether who had previously read each of the studies. Two academic had read most of the studies because few of their predictions were usable (three or fewer), all responses from these subjects were excluded. Two academic respondents said that who did not understand all of the hypotheses, so who were also excluded. This left 16 academics. Other practitioner was excluded because who said that who did not understand the instructions, which reduced the number of practitioners to 12. Six academics and one practitioner reported reading one or more studies and their responses for these studies were excluded. Finally, the predictions by expects and native subjects showed that the prediction of

consumer research percentage is larger than academics experts. For example, by assuming that researchers typically found what who were looking for and as a result, predicting
" true" for all hypotheses a subject would have been correct for 74.2% of the predictions, subjects who gave a higher percentage of these answers would be expected to achieve higher level of accuracy. Thus, consumption psychological prediction method is more effective to compare marketing research. Such as Disney entertainment theme park needs to use psychological method to predict whose visitor consumption behavior to gather what the factors can influece whose satisfied feeling to be poor after who played Disney entertainment facilities. Otherwise, in general marketing research method can only find its similar theme park competitors' strengths and weaknesses, so this method can not get the actual Disney visitors' feeling more easily.

Consumer psychological prediction method:
Can intentions Disney visitor behavior be predicted by survey research ?

How can be survey research measured that is applicable to intentions, attitude or satisfaction data to predict consumer behavior? Whether surveyed consumers will be predicted how consumers behavior are more easier than non surveyed consumers. Most academic studies of satisfaction use consumers' intention to repurchase as the criterion variable (for an exception, see Bolton 1998), and most companies rely on consumers' purchase intentions to forecast their adoption of new products or the repeat purchase of existing ones (Jamieson and Bass 1989).

In practice, some consumer psychologists' studies adjust the intention scores by analyzing that actual purchase behavior of consumers whose purchase intentions have been measured previously. For example, the popular ACNIELSEN BASES model forecasts aggregate purchase rates by applying conversion rates to measured purchase intentions (e.g. it seems that 75% of consumers who checked the top purchase-intentions box will actually purchase the product). To obtain these conversion rates, BASES uses previous studies that measured the purchase intentions of consumers and then tracked their actual purchases. However, investigating whether survey research is useful to measure consumer behavior. It has a weak point, a limitation of these studies is that companies (businessmen) focus on the internal rather than the external accuracy of purchase-intention measures. That is, the company studies measure the improvement in the ability to forecast the behavior of consumers whose intentions who previously measured for survey research experiments, not the behavior of consumers whose intentions who did not measure. Therefore, the studies assume that the companies can predict the intention-behavior relationship of non surveyed consumers on the basis of the relationship that surveyed consumer exhibit.

It would suggest that studies measure the strength of the association between intentions and behavior on the same sample of consumers overstate that external predictive accuracy of purchase intentions by survey method. This would explain why so many new products fail even after which are performed well in purchase-intention tests by survey method. I shall suggest survey framework distinguished between two sources of measurement reactivity. The first is self-generated validity effects, it is as a strengthened relationship between latent intentions and behavior, due to the measurement of intentions from post-survey research. The second source includes all measurement effects that are independent of latent intentions, such as those that social norms or post-survey intention modifications create.

I also suggest a two stage procedure to detect whether the act of measurement alters the strength of the relationship between a latent construct that is measured through surveys, experiments or observations and its consequence (e.g. intentions-behavior, attitudes-intentions, attitudes-behavior, satisfaction behavior) and to determine the time relationship in the absence of the difference between non-survey and survey consumers behavior measurement for Disney.

For example, prediction of Disney visitor's entertainment facilities choice behavior intention to find why the kind of entertainment facilities can attract more visitors choose to play in Disney theme park. Disney survey method can measure to any machine entertainment facilities. So, Disney can show the strength of the relationship between latent intentions and visitor entertainment facilities choice behavior is stronger for surveyed consumers than for similar non surveyed consumers in order to find the reasons why more visitors choose to play which kind of entertainment facilities.

I also suggest the Disney survey questions can concern to compare with other inputs factors of entertainment facilities choice decisions. e.g. personal entertainment tastes, mood, other similar entertainment theme parks' competitive environment. In order to make subsequent visiting Disney behavior is more than one time with prior intentions for every Disney old visitors. For example, Feldman and Lynch's (1988) survey method predictions, Fitzsimons and Morwitz (1996) found that measurement of general intentions to purchase automobiles increase the likelihood that buyers will repurchase the automobile brand that they also previously consume and that first time buyers will purchase brands will large market shares. Under the assumption, if the survey's result showed the automobiles brand-specific purchase intentions. Thus, Fitzsimons and Morwitz's results suggest that the measurement of general intentions increases the association between latent, brand-specific intent and brand choice. So, brand is a factor which can influence consumers to choose to buy which automobiles. In conclusion, it seems Disney can attempt to use survey method to investigate visitor entertainment facilities choice behavior to predict what factor is the most influential to attract every Disney visitor to choose to play the entertainment as well as what factor is the most influential to every Disney (re-visitor) old visitor to choose to visit Disney theme park again.

CHAPTER THREE

How social change influences student school choice

Student cost and benefit of university campus location psychological factor

Usually, students shall choose university campus is close to their houses to study. It is possible that they feel spend less time and transportation cost to go to the university campus to study that the benefit is higher. So, they will compare the cost and benefit between their house distance and university campus distance.

University can attempt to predict student individual psychological needs to avoid student turnover numbers increasing and campus location factor can influence students' studying choices. Whether University location can be a competitive advantage to attract students to study? The school (university) location means that the proximity of city center and the proximity of students home. To increase the occupancy rate, the university location is needed to provide as a model and resources based view which will be used to explain why the school location is a kind of competitive advantage for universities. According to Porter theory, it is a part of factor, which has some advantages against the treat of entry. It can decrease the treatment of rivalry. However, a good place has a certainly positive effect for attracting staff and more students. For resource-based view, the location is one of the internal resources for long term economic benefit production of factor. It can be accepted as one of the physical and tangible resource of a university.

I shall apply the first attractive factor of Porter five forces and resource based model to analyze my opinion to explain why school (university location) can influence students to choose the university to study. This view is represented by the opportunities and the threats. The university of thought is the resource based view which is represented by the strengths and weaknesses of the firm. Porter's five force model of competition elements include threats of entrants or substitutes, bargaining power of buyers or suppliers and competition rivalry. A firm's resources include brand name, in-house knowledge of technology, employment of skilled personnel, trade contract, machinery, efficient procedures and capital etc. Such as, both tangible and intangible assets are considered a firm's resources. For a university, customers can be thought as a students, suppliers can be thought as staff. In higher education industry, the good transportation infrastructure and well-connected universities have some advantages against the treat of entry to attract good staff and more students. The place of a university can decrease of treatment of rival and a good place has certainty positive location is an opportunity for universities to attract the students.

2.1 The resource based theory of university location competitive advantage

Students choose any one university to study who will judge whether economic cost is reasonable to decide to study the school, e.g. school fee, transportation cost etc.According to the Porter's theory, the resource based theory can apply competitive resources to be identifies to higher education institutions. For higher education institutions, such as resources might include the reputation of certain departments, the grouping together of areas of specialist expertise and the development of technical patents etc. Also higher education resources may not be imperfectly mobile, as the competitive resources of a university identifies tangible, intangible and organizational assets. So, the tangible resources might include campus location, building capacity, conference facilities and medical research facilities. Intangible resources generally include such items as patents, teaching and research performance, service levels and technology and the geographical location of a service. In a university, such intangible resources might include some of the above and may also include employees/ associates, e.g. experienced professors, renowned authors and distinguished teachers. Also, the location of a university can be accepted as physical and tangible resources of a university. However, I believe location is shown as an important factor to affect the students' university enrolment selection decisions.

To sources of competitive advantages are thought to be the reputation of the institution, the curriculum and educational standards, school fees (tuition), location and student activities etc. different factors. Moreover, any university's general client segments include such as, high school graduates, elderly students and international students, that have been influenced by several factors when selecting the best university to study. One of these factors is again location, the proximity to home and easy transportation is critical factor in selecting a university. Presumably, institutions that are located along well-established public transit routes have a competitive advantage over those with poor transit links. Due to the efficiency of innovation activity increased in easily accessible locations with a high density of economic activity. The existence of education and research institutions as well as easily available information is suggested as a reason for this increase. Also private higher education institutions desire to benefit from these flows by locating itself nearby. Therefore, together with other factors, such as existing capital global flows should be existing capital and population, level of income and location decisions of foundation universities. The location, social life campus, proximity of campus to the city center, exchange programs, the curricula infrastructure, languages medium of instruction and activities are the most significant factors to influence students to choose which university to study. By the past statistic indicated that the location has 94% rate, the proximity of campus to the city center has 84% rate. So, it seems the proximity of campus to the city center factor is more prior choice to compare with the school location is close to the student home factor.

Huang (2012) stated that " the right location attracts more students and ensures the revenues of the institution. The location of an educational institution might influence its future prospect of growth. A good location attracts not only more students, but also excellent teaching staff". Because of job opportunities areas, the students are able to get a part-time job and earn extra money for their tuition (Huang, 2012). Marketing concept has four "P", it can apply to university educational business, such as educational promotion, tuition price, teachers of people and school campus location of place.

Finally, I shall give two assumptions to explain why if the university location is not popular to be accepted to the country's students in general, then it will cause who won't choose to study the university. However, even if the university's tuition is reasonable or cheaper or lecturers are famous or reputation or educational advertisement is attractive. In fact, the poor location factor will influence many local or overseas students who don't choose to study the university in the country. The first assumption is that most of students feel that the proximity of the university to the city center factor affects their university final choice decision and the another assumption is that most of students feel that the proximity of university to home affects their university final choice decision. There two assumptions are used to determine the importance of university location to attract the students. In Porter theory, either proximity of city center and/or proximity of student's home of a university factors have same advantages against the treat of entry. It can decrease the treatment of rival and a good place has certainly positive effect to attract teaching staff and more students. In resource based view, the location can be accepted a kind of internal resources. It can be accepted as one of the sustainable competitive advantages literature, location is a kind of advantage for higher education institutions.

2.2 The psychological factor of student demand for alternative modes of course delivery

The factor of student demand for alternative modes of course delivery is another factor to influence the student who chooses the university to study. Any university's educational program includes program design, material production (both print and e-version), promotion, essay competition, school networks, budgeting, coordinating with various constructors, data base management and program evaluation etc.

Nowadays, university teaching methods may include face-to face, online and hybrid modes of course delivery. However, the several ways to students to deliver their course works ,such as full time, part time, internal/ non campus, external studies/distance education, summer school, winter school, semester study and trimester study. The multi site of a university , e.g. major provider of distance online education operates popular affordable learning for student to use internet to study. Although, students do not need to attend to university classroom to listen lecturer's teaching, but it can reduce face-to-face contact between lecturers and students in university classroom often.

Although, it is a technological and innovative and effective learning modalities. In fact, such new technological teaching modalities may be necessitated to the graduated or master degree or doctoral degree students. But, I feel the online teaching method is not suitable to the bachelor degree students. As the delivery of course content or the commoditization of knowledge must be re-thought to the bachelor's if the student can't enquire whose lecturer any questions to give feedback by face-to-face. Then, who will concern the course to feel more difficult possibly if who can't listen whose lecturer's opinion to solve whose challenges about the course any questions immediately in classroom often.

The second attractive factor of student demand for alternative modes of course delivery is another factor to influence the student who chooses the university to study. Nowadays, university teaching method include face to face, online and hybrid modes of course delivery. However, the several ways to students to deliver their coursework, such as full time, part time, internal/on campus, external studies/distance education, "summer school, winter school, semester study and trimester study." The multi site of a university, e.g. major popular provider of distance online education operates a flexible learning for student to use internet to study. It can reduce face to face contact between teachers and students into university classrooms. Although, it is a technological and innovative and effective learning modalities. In fact, such new technological teaching modalities may be necessitated to the graduated students or master degree or doctoral degree students. But, I feel the online teaching method is not suitable to the bachelor degree students. As the delivery of course content or the commoditization of knowledge must be re-thought to the bachelor degree students because whose knowledge level is limited if the student can't ask whose lecturer any questions by face to face contact. So, students will feel difficult to learn if who can't listen whose lecturers' teaching and to enquire any questions and to give feedback in classrooms immediately. It is possible that who will wait long time to ask many questions to prepare to wait lecturers to give feedback by email later if their lecturers use online teaching method. So it is essential that educators and administrators need to understand differentiated teaching demand to different knowledge level of students. Because student preferences may vary by age, cultural, background, degree types, learning style and matter etc. factors to decide whether whose students are suitable to teach by either online distance learning method between individual student and whose computer or face to face learning method between students and the lecturer in classroom face to face oral teaching educational method. In fact, working adults remain strongly associated eith interest in online delivery. However, the availability of evening/ weekend choices is the second most important enrollment factor to adult students, due to who consider when enrolling in an institution to indicate the important of face-to-face traditional delivery at not convenient times. So, online education is most clearly suited to independent learners those individuals who are self-motivated and self reliant and those who have a problem solving orientation.

The 2006 year Eduventures survey found that students interested in associate, bachelor's and master's degrees were most open to whole online delivery, although who were also open to campus-based delivery. Similarly, Gartner's 2008 year e-learning survey found that complete graduate programs offered online continue online. For example, international student demand for Australian higher education is expected to exceed supply in 2020 year, and key 2025 year there will be a shortfall of 22,692 international places on projected demand of 290,848. There numbers imply that to meet demand, Australian universities may want to invest further in online degree/delivery options. However, recent statistics indicate dealing interest in fully online programs in South East Asia, and a survey of 469 transnational students in 2007 year found that a majority of students opposed online provision. These findings suggest that, when branch campuses are found to be prohibitively expensive, the future of transnational programs is in programs that include face-to-face interaction facilitated by an offshore partner of the educational provider. However, education consumers prefer to combine online delivery and geographical proximity. Some of students who are living close to university campus. So who can access to courses delivered in a traditional mode, but chose to take online courses for the flexibility to it afforded them. This is an increasing trend in U.S. institutions as well, whereas online courses are used to cater solely to non-traditional students at a long distance from the campus, increasingly such classes are made available to the mainstream student constituency.

2.3 Whether online and hybrid courses will influence to university students to choose the university to study.

How can the technology online teaching contributing improve student outcome? At least, learning outcomes for students in online and hybrid courses match those of students in traditional settings. When these are reasons to believe that the hybrid model would produce more effective learning outcomes than the fully-online model in theory. Also evidence suggests that e-learning continues to grow in popularity with the number of hybrid or blended courses increasing at the fastest rate, although online/hybrid courses certainly do not outcomes courses presented the traditional (i.e. face-to-face traditional classroom) delivery method. These facts help to demonstrate that despite the popularity and increased availability of online courses. However, students still value traditional classroom methods and that online options may not significantly detract from on-campus enrollments.

Hybrid degree programs, also known as blended programs are courses of study that combine traditional classroom based instruction with significant amounts of online instruction, with each passing semester, hybrid degree programs become increasingly popular for students and universities alike. Such courses allow students to reduce time-consuming trips to campus when still benefiting from face-to-face teaching method allow colleges and universities to more effectively use classroom space and to reduce cost. For these reasons, hybrid courses are often praised as the best of both classroom and online teaching methods, it is possible that students have chance to go to classroom to listen lecturer's teaching and who also have chance to use internet to learn from online teaching method as the same time. These is no standard model for hybrid education. Some programs may have students split their time evenly between online and on-campus instruction; some may have students complete the majority of their work online with occasional intensive weekends of on-campus activity and some require students to enroll in a combination of traditional classes as well as strictly online classes. Nowadays, a major educational consulting group found that hybrid or blended learning was the most rapidly growing delivery option when online, hybrid and traditional delivery options were taken into acount. Because of the trend towards more hybrid programming, university officials concern on their potential impact on enrollment levels for on-campus degree programs. Some speculate that hybrid programs have the potential to overtake traditional programs, when others hope to use hybrid programs as stepping stones to attract more students to campus on a full time basis. The structures of different programs reflect institutions‘ intent to use hybrid programs to attract students from non-traditional areas. For example, Michigam State university's Master of social work hybrid program accepts roughly 25 students per year. In 2008 year, these students lived anywhere from 85 to 435 miles from the main campus, therefore frequent in person activities were not feasible. Gather in addition to completing online assignments, students attended a one-week-summer institute on campus in June and face-to-face instruction sessions in smaller groups organized by geography once per month during the fall and spring semesters. In short, hybrid programs do not necessarily replace on-campus offerings, nor do they commonly draw more students to campus on a full time basis. Rather, they complement existing program offerings by reaching out to new packets of students who have the mean to visit campus on occasion but not regularly.

In conclusion, any university ought follow its subjects, student age, school location and tuition, lecturers' repuation and school research facilities etc. factors to decide whether the course is suitable to be chose either online teaching or face-to-face traditional classroom teaching or hybrid (online and face-to-face both) teaching method to teach whose different degree level students. Because these factors will influence who to choose which kind of subjects to study. For example, if many first year students feel the subjects are difficult to learn. It implies that online distance teaching or hybrid teaching method is not suitable to be taught to them. The traditional face-to-face contact traditional classroom teaching method is more suitable to be taught to them. So, it is flexible to any one of these teaching method to choose to teach any subjects to university student. It is no absolute suitable teaching method to teach any one of subject in any one of university. Because any university is independent, it means that the teaching method is suitable to be taught to the students in the university. It doesn't mean that the same teaching method is suitable to be taught to the students to another university because every university's lecturer's reputation, school tuition fee, course's contents and qualities and student age segment and location is different among of them. It is very difficult to ensure which kind of teaching method must be suitable to be taught to the subject to all universities in any countries. Thus, if the university can predict which student individual psychology needs, then it can reduce its student turnover number successfully.

In conclusion, in behavioral economy view point, consumer decision making has long been of interest to research. Such as this university student choice factor, e.g. university location, course design etc. factors can influence students to choose which university to study. The most prevalent model from this perspective is " utility theory" which proposes that consumers make choices based on the expected outcomes of their decisions. Some consumption psychologists view consumers are as rational decision makers and who are only concerned with self interest. However, utility theory views the consumer as a rational economic man. Consumer behavior considers a wide range of factors how to influence to change the consumer behavior , and acknowledges a board range of consumption activities beyond purchasing.

These activities commonly include need recognition, information search, evaluation of alternatives, the building of purchasing intention, the act of purchasing, consumption and final disposal. Some psychologists regard man and rational and self interested, making decisions based upon the ability to maximize utility when spending the minimum effort.

It concerns economic man theory, in order to behavior rationally in the economic sense, as consumers must aware of all the available consumption options be capable of correctly rating each alternative and be available to select the optimum course of action. Some psychologists view point, behavior is subject to biological influence through instinctive force or drives with act outside of conscious thought. So, the consumption psychological behavior is determined by biological drives, rather than individual cognition, or environmental stimuli thoughts and feelings can be regarded as consumer behaviors.

Some psychologists feel environmental variables influence consumer behaviors. However, an influential role of the environment and social experience is acknowledged with consumers activity seeking and receiving environmental and stimuli is as informational inputs aiding internal decision making . Input variables are the environmental stimuli that consumer is subjected to influence to choose either to buy or not buy the product, e.g. brand, advertisement, price, sale channel, place, salespeople service, quality, loyalty, durability etc. different elements can influence consumer final decision making. This variable factors can influence any university students' choices, such as the university is famous or not famous, how the university advertise its education, what is the university school fee for every different kind of degree, where is the university location, e.g. city or countryside etc. different psychological and economy factors.

Research questions

(1) Whether has it relationship between behavioral economy and consumer psychology ?

(2) Can apply behavioral economy concept to predict consumer behavior?

(3) How can apply behavioral economy concept to predict consumer behavior?

Research question answers

Economy and psychological factors predict consumer behavior

Some investigations indicated about the changes in consumer behavior are caused by external environment influences, e.g. globalization and development of information technologies. It can help to understand the specific factors what should be taken into account in evaluation of consumer behavior.

In macroeconomic environment view point, for example, the global trend of economic liberalization, new political geography, gradual removal of international trade barriers , rapid technological advancement these environmental factors are just a few of the factors that have had major effect on the business management practices nowadays. The most obvious impact on the practical level of doing business has these macroeconomic environmental factors intensified competition. So, these factors can influence micro economical consumer behavior indirectly. Consumer behavior is mix of elements from psychology, sociology, sociopsychology, anthropology and economic. Management process will identifies, anticipates and supplies customer requirement efficiently and profitably.

In consumption psychological view point, technical criteria concerns the cost aspects of purchase, durability, reliability, comfort and convenience. Economic criteria concerns the cost aspects of purchase, include price, running costs and residual values, e.g. a trade in value of a car.

In conclusion, economic environmental and consumption psychological factors can influence consumer behavior changing, so businessmen can attempt to do any surveys, experiment etc. research methods to predict how consumer behavior will change to attract them to choose to buy their products more easily.

CHAPTER FOUR

How social change influences airline passenger need change

How can airline gas or oil price influence passenger individual airline choice?

If the global oil price increased, then it will be possible to influence global airlines to increase their air tickets price. Finally, global oil price raising factor will cause global airlines' air ticket prices to be increased to influence global traveller number to be decreased.

For airline industry, if the airline firm can predict global economy trend how to influence oil or gas price, then it can predict its passenger consumption of choice more easily. Due to we are entering globalization. In Special, airline transportation demands are also increasing, due to many travelers need to catch planes to travel as well as many cargoes need to be carried to planes to transport to different countries to sell. It seems aviation transportation industry is important to influence the health of the global economy growth nowadays. However, ignorance of internal or external market dynamics, catching travelers business can be detrimental to airline profitability more than carrying cargoes business. Because the demands of travelling different countries' travelers' consumption are still more than the demands of businessmen carrying cargoes in any countries every year. So, the passenger income sector is still have the important position to compare to cargo income sector in global airline transportation industry any countries nowadays.

How can negative social change influence any airlines' air ticket prices to be risen to influence cost raising? In fact, the increase in petroleum price can have chance to affect airlines in a negative manner because increased oil prices have resulted in the reduction of services operations, the number of airline schedules flights, even airline bankruptcies. Whether inflation, terrorism, oil price, bank interest rate etc. external factors have the most influential to cause the bad effects to cause airlines need to raise air ticket price to influence traveler numbers to be decreased.

To support this hypotheses, these are my research questions, such as : Does a combination of terrorism and price of petroleum significantly influence airline profit changing mostly? The alternative hypothesis was whether a significant relationship exists between terrorism, price of petroleum and airline profitability more than other factors, such as inflation, bank interest rate of these factors cause to ticket price raising. I shall indicate that the first assumption was that terrorism has a negative effect on airline profitability and another assumption was that only external factors as oil prices or terrorism affect airline profitability.

3.1 What is the relationship of oil price and terrorism to airline industry to influence ticket price increasing?

Terrorism is one negative psychological factor to influence the travellers who choose to travel to the country. However the effects of oil price and terrorism on airline profitability was limited to a regional perspective, e.g. the terrorism attack of plane crash event to USA on 11 Sept. After the terrorism attack happened on USA 11 Sept. incident of terrorism attack was restricted to events of skyjacking, attacks on oil production, refinery and distribution. Other types of terrorist activities, such as attacks on financial targets or senior government officials could have an adverse effect on the petroleum and airline industry. I think the disruption of the production or distribution of petroleum because of incidents of terrorism was costly in terms of loss of business and the inflationary effect on fuel dependent products or services.

In fact, some airlines have adopted more fuel saving technology, so whose fuel consumption would not use more than other non fuel saving technology airlines, these own fuel saving technology airlines which do not need to increase ticket prices to influence passenger numbers to be decreased in possible. It seems fuel price increasing will not be the only factor to influence the airline industry's traveler numbers decreasing, in addition to terrorism external incident factor influence. However, due to some airlines which have fuel saving technology, so which can avoid to use more fuel to provide planes to use and which fuel costs will be reduced, then which can provide cheaper air ticket fare prices to compare the non fuel saving technology airlines. The result will cause some airlines will lose travelling customers in this global airline travelling market, also the non fuel saving technology airlines need to renew their fuel technology if which want to keep their competitive abilities to avoid to close down their businesses.

Also, I shall indicate the financial risk of airline industry evidence from Cathay Pacific airways and China airlines against key determinants of which include interest rate, exchange rate and fuel price risk for the period of January 1996 year to December 2011 year. During this period, these key external factors which were the most serious influence to cause these two airlines choose to change their strategic behaviors. Due to any these financial risks is difficult to predict and it was also changing often, these factors will also affect any airlines stock returns which arise from changing economic conditions, e.g. fuel price movements and fluctuations in exchange rates. These external unpredicted changing factors will attribute to the air tickets cyclical demand, capital investment, fixed costs of labor and landing rights to this global airline industry.

However, the relationship between fuel price and stock prices varies across economies. The effects of oil price changes in sub-sector indices, such as wood, paper and printing, insurance and electricity. In the past, on global stock exchange market was positively significant in 2011 year. Otherwise, with respect to the U.S.A. aviation industry, some economists suggested that global airlines stock returns were negatively to percentage change in fuel prices related to any airline firm value, e.g. Qantas and Air New Zealand were negatively share price growth to fuel price risk in the short term in the 2011 year. Thus, airline industy needs to concern whether the effects of oil price changes in sub-sector indices, such as wood, paper and printing, insurance and electricity influences to predict when oil price will increase or decrease because it will lead to influence its passenger travelling numbers indirectly and these sub-sector industries have close relationship to bring cause and effect influence to oil price to airline industry.

3.2 How can demand be caused by e-service transaction channel to predict passenger individual consumption choice for airline industry?

It is one travel sale psychological behavior which can influence the traveller number increases or decreases to the travel agent or airline. Electronic airline ticket shopping is one good example for passengers' consumption behavioral influence. In the past, if somebody wanted to buy a book, on little learned about from whose friends or relatives, first who had to go into more bookstores to see of that book exists and after to make some price comparisons in order to decide from where to buy it from one bookstore choice only. These activities were time and money consuming. The situation has changed how the person can learn about launching a book easily from social networks, and by simply accessing an online store, such as Amazon . com , readers who can purchase the book to save time and energy by pressing a button activity only. So, the process of buying a product simplified in terms of time and money spent, but because more difficult in terms of decision making which has become more complex. The main reason is people have too many options to choose from in terms of product or service, price, quality and time.

Can digital internet technological electronic service influence consumers to choose this shopping style when who is habit to spend time to play internet . Is lifestyle a tool for understanding buyer behavior? Consumption psychologists had examined to confirm that it has relationship between the consumers' general life styles and their consumption pattern and the brands of products are used by them. They concluded that consumers often choose products, service and others because who are associated with a certain lifestyle . The products are the building blocks of lifestyle, marketers should therefore, have a complete idea of these changing lifestyles. So, dividing to segment them and position their products succcssfully.

The lifestyle of individuals has always been of great interest to marketers. They deal with everyday behaviorally oriented facets of people as well as their feelings, attitudes, interests and opinions. A lifestyle marketing perspective recognize that people sort themselves into groups on the basis of the things groups on the basis of the things who like to do, how who like to spend their leisure time and how who choose to spend their disposable income. Lifestyle is an important concept used in segmenting markets and understanding target customers, which is not provided by the study of demographics alone.

Many researchers have focused on identifying the lifestyle of the consumers to have better information about them. This study used the lifestyle analysis to identify market segments. Otherwise, some consumption psychologists believe to apply life style analysis for market segmentation, the developed of product strategy and the developed of the most appropriate communication strategy. They suggested successful retailers based on general application of lifestyle analysis have begun to implement a portfolio management approach which focuses on the needs of the key target markets. So, lifestyle segmentation can provide a valuable insight into the task of creating an effective brand identity. The study of lifestyle often provides fresh insights into the market and gives a more dimensional view of the target consumers. The marketing managers may be able to develop improved multi-dimensional views of key market segments, uncover new product opportunities obtain better product position, develop improved advertising communications based on a richer more life-like portrait of the target consumer and generally improve overall marketing strategy. These consumption psychologists assume that the members of any target client groups are all similar. The first hypothesis is people differ in their lifestyle they can be grouped into segments and the second hypothesis is people belonging to lifestyle segments differ in their demographics.

Thus, such as airline ticket every consumer who can either choose to buy electronic airline ticket from internet or airline shop. In travel consumption environment, a travel consumer chooses a travel agent package or a airline brand , which indicates a maximum possibility of the definition of whose lifestyle identity. Alternatively, a travelling person makes a choice in a travel consumption environment in order to define actualize whose lifestyle identity if through the travel agent package products or airline brands chosen. It can be assumed that the travelling individual's consumption behavior can be predicted from an understanding of how who represents whose would be himself/ herself of the details of choosing lifestyle system are known from internet survey or questionnaire method. Thus, digital internet is one good channel to research travel consumer lifestyle to predict whose consumption style.

In economic view point, demand is a model of travel consumer behavior. It attempts to identify the factors that influence the choices that are made by travel consumers. In microeconomics, the objective of the travel consumer is to maximize the utility that can be derive given their travel choice preferences, income, the airline ticket prices relates travel package products and services for which the travel demand function in derived.

Utility is the capacity of a travel package product or service to satisfy a traveller' want. It can explain the phenomenon of travelling value. Since utility is subjective and can't be observed and measured directly. The objective in microeconomics is to maximize the satisfaction or utility of traveller individuals given their travel package preferences, incomes and the airline ticket prices of travel package products or services who buy or consume in travel market. Thus, total travel utility of more or less travel satisfaction degree be caused by traveller consumer behavior. It is the traveller consumption psychological result (effect) and it has close relationship with travel agent service.

Are internet delivered electronic services being made available to travel consumers about how who are evaluated for travel airline potential adoption to predict travel consumer behavior? Some psychologists' past researches had focused primary on the positive travel utility gains attributable to information technology adoption. However, their results indicate that e-service is adversely affect primary be performance-based risk perceptions, when perceived ease of use of the e-service reduces risk perceptions. E-services are interactive software based information systems received via internet. E-services are important in travel agent/airline e-ticket business to consumer (B2C) e airline ticket-commerce because which represent ways to provide on travel demand solutions and improving travel customer satisfaction. So, it brings this question shows that whether travel agent/airline businessmen can predict travel consumer adoption of e-services.

It is important to distinguish the different between conducting basic travel e-ticket purchase transactions and adopting e-service. The travel ticket e-service adoption decision is essentially different from most typical travel ticket e-commerce purchases as which create a longer-term relationship between the travel consumer and travel service provider. Hence, even, if travel ticket e-services are an e-commerce application to which some adoption models exists. It requires a distinct conceptualization to travel e-ticket businessmen and traditional travel agent businessmen need focuses on the role of perceived risk on influencing on adopting intentions of travel ticket e-services. When travel ticket e-services are convenient and create efficiencies for travel ticket e-businessmen users. Little is understand about how travel consumers evaluate them for adoption. So, travel ticket e-service performance quality and the potential utility of the travel service usefulness is a difficult task for travel consumers, especially given the newness of the online e-ticket visa card payment environment. If the travel consumer feels e-transaction is not suitable to him/her to use for airline ticket shopping, then it is possible that it will reduce the chance to the travel consumer to choose to use the kind of e-transaction service to buy the airline brand of travel package products. So, this travel e-service transaction will include both risks (potential negotiations utility) and perceived usefulness (potential positive utility) to let every travel customer to feel either of high utility or low utility after who choose to use e-service to buy airline ticket shopping.

How important are risk perceptions to the overall travel e-services adoption decision? What types of risk are influenced and therefore important to the travel customer of e-service? Perceived risk is commonly thought of as an uncertainty regarding possible negative consequences of using a travel package product or service. It has formally been defined as " a combination of uncertainty plus service of outcome involved" (Bauer 1960, 1967) and " the expectation of losses associates with purchase and acts as an inhibitor to purchase behavior" (Peter & Ryam 1976). Their research's pilot test result have indicated some electronic service shoppers, such as airline e-ticket buyers concern for the theft of their private information, or simply its misuse by the travel businessmen collecting it. Members of a focus group drawn from the population studied to concern for the loss of privacy of personal financial information as an identify-theft. So, privacy risk was gathered and modeled as a deterrent to utility evaluations and the adoption choice to influence consumers choices to buy the product from this e-service sale channel.

Overall, some consumers will feel those perceived risks to influence who decide to buy the travel ticket package product from e-service sale channel. Such as performance risk, it means the possibility of the product manufacturing and not performing as it was designed and advertised and failing to deliver the desired benefits, financial risk, it means the potential monetary outlet associated with the initial purchase price as well as the subsequent maintenance cost of the travel package product (ibid). The current financial services include potential for financial loss , due to fraud, time with means travel consumers may lose time when making a bad purchasing decision by wasting time researching and making the purchased, learning ow to use a product or service only to have to replace if it does not perform to expectations, psychological risk means potential loss of self oneself. Travel consumers feel unwise if they experience a non-performing travel package products and may experience their feelings of harm to their self-image from the frustration of not achieve their buying goals, social risk means potential loss of status in one's social group as a result of adopting a travel package product or service, looking foolish, privacy risk means potential loss of control over personal information, such as when information about travel package purchase used without the travel customer's knowledge or permission. A travel consumer is carrying a criminal use whose identity to perform fraudulent transactions. Overall , when any one consumer feels one of those perceived risk will occur, then any one of these risks will influence who to choose to use e-service transactions method to buy travel package product from internet. So, travel package internet shopping seems have bad image to influence travel consumer shopping choice of channel as well as travel consumer demand of the travel package product will be reduced if who feel e-ticekt service transaction channel is not safe to whom.

Is online video and television service is to be affective in predicting technology adoption to influence consumption behavior choice? It seems online video and television and online e-ticket travel package service which are similar to behavioral economy analysis. Such as the online entertainment consumer who can use computer to watch online video and television in anywhere, e.g.

library, at home etc. places. Even some online video and television service can provide free charge to let any entertainment consumer to watch any time from internet. So, who will feel no any expense. Online e-ticket buying service can let the travel consumer use whose computer to compare any airline companies' e-tickets prices and travel date and time schedule and travel destination from internet at home conveniently. So, who does not need to spend transportation cost or driver whose car to to to the travel agent or airline to buy paper airline ticket. Hence, both online video and television rent service and e-airline ticket consumption services can help consumers spend less time and expense to make consumption decision at home in short time. It is a popular online consumption behavioral economy model.

Nowadays, online video and television services have become one of the most promising activities in terms of advertising revenue. E-Marketer has estimated that online video or television advertising will soar at 56% to 70% in the next five years (Halleman, 2008). To predict user acceptance of online video and television services. Despite a digital growth in online video and television to service over the span of a few years.

What factors can influence consumers to choose to buy the product after who watch online video and television advertising? Some psychological experiments shows a greater influence of perceived behavioral control on intention to use this type of services. The effects of attitude toward use and subjective norm were positive, but more moderate. The lesser effect of attitude towards use may be explained by the evidence benefits of watching videos online. However, search recent consumer studies have confirmed that watching online videos and televisions has become one of the favorite online activities for internet users (Hallerman 2008. Mulligan et al. 2008).

Hence, airline ticket consumer individual behavior can apply e-service questionnaires survey channel to gather what who needs or expectation are chosen to buy any prefer airlines to predict how to satisfy or attract whom final travel consumption of decision more easily.

3.3 Can advertising influence consumption behavior?

Advertising is one consumer psychological method to influence consumer number to be increased or decreased to any travel agents or airlines. Advertising is a subject on which people tend to hold strong and often opposing views, and economists are not expectations to this. Some economists regard advertising as one means by which firms concentrate on promoting whose tastes and opinions in the direction of their products and also more generally in favor of private consumption (consumer behavior). Other economists see advertising as an efficient way by which firms supply information to potential consumers. Otherwise, some economists see advertising as a barrier inhibiting new entrants into an industry thereby enabling the established firms to reap high profits, when others see advertising as evidence of competition and an aid to new entrants in establishing themselves. So, it seems advertising can influence consumer choices possibly.

Advertising relatives to sales varies considerably between industries. For example, the ratio of advertising in 1968 year varied from over 15% in the toilet preparations industry to over 10% in the soap and detergents industry to near is in a number of toilet preparation producer industries. A distinction is frequently made between information an persuasive advertising , and it is often suggested that some forms of advertising (such as classified ads.) are likely to have more informative content than other forms (such as television advertising).

What is the sale of advertising in the demand function? One response is that a firm can sell more of its products because consumers have more information on that product. The information may relate to its existence, price, quality etc. Thus advertising is seen as essentially supplying information to consumers how to choose the similar kinds of products to decide which is the suitable product to buy. The other response is that advertising seeks to persuade consumers to purchase with favored people or situations, repetition of the same message. This advertising seeks to promote tastes rather than to inform. One firms' advertising may not be successful through false judgement by that firm and its advertisers or because of the impact of the advertising of other firms. The difference between the two responses can be put in terms of the conventional; utility maximization approach top consumer demand theory. The first response regards consumers' taste (i.e. the utility function) as fixed and advertising informs the consumer about availability, price etc. So, that utility maximizing process can take place more effectively . The second response regards advertising and seeking to promote consumers' tastes and change the consumers' utility function in a manner favorable to the advertiser. So, different types of advertising have been as containing information and persuasion in varying proportions and varying in the degree of desirability. But for the firm, the intention is to sell its products, and it will present any information in a way which seeks to influence the consumer to purchase its products.

Some consumption psychologists believe utility maximization by well-informed individuals plays a central role in conventional micro-economies. However, advertising can be a part of the conduct of firms in that firms use advertising amongst many other things to seek to increase profits or whatever their objectives it. Finally, advertising can be a part of performance, influenced by industrial structure. Some consumption psychologists also believe the highly differentiated products are more suitable for advertising than undifferentiated ones. They suppose existing firms benefit from their past investment in advertising and new entrants have to overcome those advantage.

If advertising is a profitable activity for firms to undertake, then the question arises as to why other firms don't follow suit. If other firms possibly including new entrants did follow suit, then the returns to advertising are likely to be reduced. It is useful to discuss the returns to advertising in terms of the returns in increased sales per advertising message and the cost of delivering an advertising message. Increasing return would occur form a message of repeated showing of a particular advertisement led to the product demand increasing at an increasing rate. Thus, of the product demand per unit of time is same to the number of advertising message per unit of time, then increasing sale returns would be raised possibly. The implications of any increasing sale returns to advertising may depend upon whether the increasing returns operate for advertising of a single product or for advertising of a number of products. Thus, it seems advertising promotion behavior can create barriers to entry to reduce consumers have more choices from other competitors' similar products sale. Such as any airline businesses can attempt to use advertising to attract travellers to concern what they can give different or unique or excellent airline service to let travellers feel which airline service is more especial to compare other airline competitors, during external environment factor influence consumer travel desire , such as fuel rising or unemployment etc. external poor environment factor influence to global airline travel market. Hence, airline advertising promotion method can let travellers to feel why (what reasons) who ought to find the airline travelling service.

3.4 How can airline atmosphere environment influence traveller travel choice behavior?

It is one macro positive or negative economic external environment factor influence global airline traveller number. On the one hand, some consumption psychologists suggest in-store variable factor can influence consumer emotion to feel either pleasure or displeasure of intended shopping behaviors within the store, thus these consumption psychologists who believe retail store environment can influence consumption behavior. On the other hand, some employment psychologists also suggest work environment can influence employee individual emotion to work, work environment include hospitals, schools and prisons etc. public work environment. It seems consumers and employees whose emotion will be influenced by environment factor. It brings this question. Can store atmosphere environment predict consumers buying decision?

These consumption psychologists feel the component of store image, physical in-store variable , such as aisle width, brightness and crowding, when clearly these physical variables are store environment's major factor which can influence consumption behavior will be changed. Some retailers have claimed large effects from manipulating store atmosphere via layout, lighting, color and music (Wysocki 1979; Stevens 1980).

Some consumption psychologists also show these avoidance behaviors can cause consumer individual shopping emotion. First, physical approach and avoidance, which can be related to store patronage intentions at a basic level. Exploratory approach and avoidance can be related to in-store search and exposure to a broad or narrow range of retail offerings. Second, Communication approach and avoidance can be related to interaction with sales personnel and floor staff. Third, performance and satisfaction approach and avoidance can be related to repeat shopping frequency as well as reinforcement of time and money expenditures in the store.

In consumer psychological view point, pleasure or displeasure refers to the degree to which the consumer feels good, joyful, happy or satisfied in the situation. Then, another degree to which a consumer feels excited, stimulated, alert or active in the situation. Thus, if the consumer feels the shopping environment is comfortable, joyful, happy or satisfied. The shopping environment, it will have more chance to influence the consumer chooses shopping. Otherwise if, the consumer feels the shopping environment is excited, alert, stimulated or active. The shopping environment will have less chance to influence the consumer chooses shopping. It seems each consumer individual emotion will influence whose consumption behavior as well as store atmosphere environment has close relationship to influence each consumer individual emotion also.

Thus, retailers need to concern how to design whose store environment, e.g. what kind of furniture color, style and size; how much area of the store. For example, the store area is either large or middle or small area to let many or small number of consumers to stay in the store at the same time. How to let consumers to enter or leave the store? For example, how to let consumers to feel to leave the store easily when the fire is happening in store, it can make the consumers feel more safe, so who will have more probable to stay in the store to consume. How to display whose products to let consumers feel to touch or see to find any products on the shelves more easily. Choosing what kind of music to let consumers to listen during who are staying to shopping in store, e.g. soft music or none any music (quiet environment). These different store external feeling factors will influence each consumer individual emotion to feel more comfortable or uncomfortablc feeling to decide to spend more long time or short time to stay in the store. Thus, it seems store atmosphere environment can influence consumer individual shopping behavior, so retailers can not neglect how to design store atmosphere environment to let whose customers feel more comfortable and safe to stay in stores.

Hence, it seems that if any airline company which can design attractive service counter environment to let travellers feel the airline service counter comfortable and enjoyable. It will have possible to influence them to choose to buy any travel package service from the attractive airline atmosphere environment influence more easily. So, atmosphere environment has indirect factor to influence consumer to consume more easily.

3.5 How can airline counter servicer knowledge influence traveller consumption behavior?

It is the airline consumer service psychological factor to influence its traveller number. Can model for understanding service encounter evaluation that can synthesize consumer satisfaction, services marketing, and attribution to influence consumption behavior to the retailer? Can airline servicer travel knowledge and service attitude influence traveller consumption of decison making ? These factors concern on the service industries how to influence consumption behavior, which focus on service encounter satisfaction and service quality to both the importance and the complexity of the issues. First and foremost, customer satisfaction depends directly and most immediately on the management and monitoring of individual service encounters (Parasuraman, Zeithaml, and Berry 1985; Shostack 1984, 1987; Sollmon et al. 1985).

What is the conceptual definition of service encounter? The model of service encounter evaluation relies on Shostack's (1985, p.243) definition of the term" service encounter" as " a period of time during which a consumer directly interacts with a service." The author identified all aspects of the service firm with which the consumer may interact, including its personnel, its physical facilities and other tangible elements, during a given period of time. I give this hypothesis, such as when an employee offers to compensate the customer for service failure, the offer may influence attributions. The employee performance will lead the customer to have negative beliefs about the firm, when the bad employee offer leads the customer to think bad image to the firm. So, the employee's bad service attitude can influence the offer is made to compensate for service failure to build bad service image to the company. Moreover, physical surroundings also are hypothesized to influence customer emotion in service failure situations. For example, if a customer experiences service failure in an organized , professional environment, e.g. lawyer, doctor, accountant professional services. The customer may not have more confidence to find the firm to serve to him again. In contrast, in a disorganized environment, the physical cues may suggest incompetence, inefficiency and poor service. In such an environment, the customer may attribute greater responsibility to the firm and be more likely to expect the same type of problem to occur in the future. Thus, any professional service firms, whose employees' service performance can influence customers' confidence to decide to find whose professionals to give any professional service opinions again. Thus, any professional service firm, whose employees' service performance can influence customers' confidence to the service firm likely.

How can the impact of personality and emotion on post-purchase service processes influence consumption behavior? Will consumption behavior be influenced to the retailer by consumer satisfaction or dissatisfaction and post-purchase service behaviors? Such as complaints, recommendations, and repeat purchase intentions, toward loyalty and word of mouth. Developing a new customer is expensive. Particularly in mature markets, competition is strong, product differentiation is low, and promotional costs have skyrocketed. So, understanding who these customers are, why who are dissatisfied, and how or even whether to market to them is an increasingly important issue.

That a customer's level of satisfaction affects much post-purchase behaviors, such as complaining and negative word of mouth is well documented. Satisfaction itself is influenced by comparing actual product performance to expectation. So, some consumption actual product performance will be needed to expectations by the product manufacuter or seller. So, some consumption psychologists began to research that the role of consumption based emotion in consumer satisfaction formation how to make recent personality research particularly concerning. It seems post-purchase processed can be a response to influence consumption- based emotions and consumption behavior to any retailers. The degree of satisfaction is a specific consumption experience, it has a direct impact on such post-purchase processes as repeat purchase intentions and complaining. So, any retailers need to concern on how predicting post-purchase consumer behavior will be.

Because personality should be an important predictor of consumption experiences, and thereby of post-purchase processes. Post-purchase processes can include either on positive consumption-based emotions or on negative consumption-based emotions. When the consumer satisfies to use the product, the useful of product expectation will be increased. Otherwise, when the consumer dissatisfies to use the product, the useful of product expectation will be decreased and the consumer complaint behavior will be increased. So, it seems post-purchase processes can influence consumers to decide to continue to choose to buy the products from the retailer again as well as how to reduce consumers have negative emotions to the products which is an important factor to influence any consumption behavior changing to the retailer. Hence, airline or travel agent counter servicer's attitude and travel knowledge will have either positive or negative influence to any traveller's final travel decision.

3.6 In -store consumer digital signage behavior how can influence consumer behavior

It is one payment method to influence traveller individual choice to the travel agent. Digital signage is a new technology, where people broadcasting displays adapt their content to the audience demographic and features. In some shopping centers, retailers like to use machine learning methods on real-world digital signage viewer data to predict consumer behavior in a retail environment. Digital signage systems are nowadays primarily used as public information interfaces. They display general information, advertise content or serve as media for enhanced customer experience.

Interaction design studies show that the interaction level of users with digital signage systems will increase, including also the mobility of users around the display. Since digital signage systems can have a significant effect on commerce, which are also rapidly shopping centers ad retail stores. Retail generalization studies reveal that in-store digital signage increases customer traffic and sales (Burke, 2009).

Some consumer psychologists believe purchase decision processes can be described with five stages. The first stage is problem recognition, where consumer recognizes a problem is a need. The second stage is search for information via heightened attention of consumer towards information about a certain product, which can even resolve in actual proactive search for information. The third stage represents the evaluation of alternatives , which usually involves a comparison between various options and features based in the models of the expected value and beliefs. In the fourth stage of the purchase decision process, a provider, place, time, value , type and quality of the selected product or service and determined. The fifth stage are the final stage describes the post purchase use, behavior and actions.

Why will digital signage influence consumers choose to buy the product? It is possible that some consumers who like to use visa card to go to shopping as well as who like to use digital signage to confirm who are the visa card holders to let the businessmen to feel who are rich to let bank give trust to issue visa card to them to use. So, who do not need to bring much money to leave home to prepare to buy anything and who only bring one visa card to leave home safely. Thus, the digital signage systems are a new approach to automatic modelling of in-store consumer behavior based on audience measurement data. It is a unique machine payment method, which can also be used to predict more distinctive characteristics, such as an consumer individual's role in the purchase decision process. So, I believe digital signage audience measurement data can be used to model various user behavior for one kind of in-store consumer behavior prediction of method. Hence, it seems travel agent or airline can choose to apply visa card signature method to encourage travellers to make travel package purchase decision more easily by this electronic card payment method.

Printed by Libri Plureos GmbH in Hamburg,
Germany